Practical Travel

GRAN CANARIA
(SPAIN)

GW00367806

1992

Hayit Publishing

Using this Book

Books in the *Practical Travel* series offer a wealth of practical information. You will find the most important tips for your travels conveniently arranged in alphabetical order. Cross-references aid in orientation so that even entries which are not covered in depth, for instance "Holiday Apartments," lead you to the appropriate entry, in this case "Accommodation." Also thematically altered entries are also cross-referenced. For example under the heading "Medication," there appear the following references: "Medical Care," "Pharmacies," "Vaccinations."

With travel guides from the *Practical Travel* series the information is already available before you depart on your trip. Thus, you are already familiar with necessary travel documents and maps, even customs regulations. Travel within the country is made easier through comprehensive presentation of public transportation, car rentals in addition to the practical tips ranging from medical assistance to newspapers available in the country. The descriptions of cities are arranged alphabetically as well and include the most important facts about the particular city, its history and a summary of significant sights. In addition, these entries include a wealth of practical tips — from shopping, restaurants and accommodation to important local addresses. Background information does not come up short either. You will find interesting information about the people and their culture as well as the regional geography, history and current political and economic situation.

As a particular service to our readers, *Practical Travel* includes prices in hard currencies so that they might gain a more accurate impression of prices even in countries with high rates of inflation. Most prices quoted in this book have been converted to US$ and £.

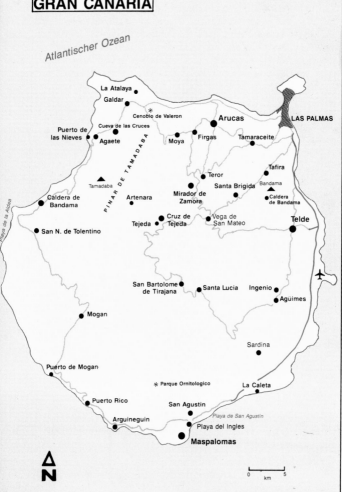

GRAN CANARIA

Atlantischer Ozean

LAS PALMAS

La Atalaya
Galdar
* Cenobio de Valeron
Arucas
Puerto de las Nieves
Cueva de las Cruces
Agaete
Moya
Firgas
Tamaraceite
Teror
Tafira
PINAR DE TAMADABA
Tamadaba
Mirador de Zamora
Santa Brigida
Bandama
Artenara
Caldera de Bandama
Caldera de Bandama
Tejeda
Cruz de Tejeda
Vega de San Mateo
Telde
San N. de Tolentino
Playa de la Aldea
San Bartolome de Tirajana
Santa Lucia
Ingenio
Agüimes
Mogan
Sardina
Puerto de Mogan
* Parque Ornitologico
La Caleta
Puerto Rico
San Agustin
Playa de San Agustin
Arguineguin
Playa del Ingles
Maspalomas

N

0   km   5

[1st] Edition 1992
UK Edition: ISBN 1 874251 35 5
US Edition: ISBN 1 56634 003 9

© copyright 1992 UK Edition: Hayit Publishing GB, Ltd, London
    US Edition: Hayit Publishing USA, Inc., New York

© copyright 1991 original version: Hayit Verlag Gmbh
    Cologne/Germany

Author: Peter Kensok
Translation, Adaption, Revision: Scott Reznik
Print: Druckhaus Cramer, Greven/Germany
Photography: Peter Kensok, Renate Tarrach, Spanish Tourism
Administration
Maps: Ralf Tito

Contents

Accommodation

Spain is well organised in terms of tourism — this is especially true regarding accommodation. The Tourist Information Offices (→ *Tourist Information*) will send lists of hotels, campsites and apartments in various regions upon request. When sent directly from the Tourist Information Offices, these lists are usually up-to-date including the most current prices.

Information on the Canary Islands may not be the most current, and one can be surprised by an enormous price increase. This, however, is a result of the high rate of inflation. The actual price per night is posted on a table at every officially recognised accommodation.

Whether private accommodation or hotel, the premises are inspected and the result is posted next to or above the main entrance. The following are the various categories of accommodation available in Spain:

AT = Apartementos. Apartments are fully furnished with one or two bedrooms, a shower or bath, and usually a kitchenette or even a living room. This category is subdivided according to the number of keys:

Mountains in the Agaete region

One key — here there is usually hot water or a shower and a lift in buildings with more than four floors.

Two keys — there is a house telephone at the reception, hot water on every floor, heating and lifts in buildings with more than three floors.

Three keys — heating, hot water, lifts in buildings with more than three floors, reception area, telephone calls can be connected to each apartment.

Four keys — luxury category. Air conditioning, lifts in buildings with more than two floors, heating, hot water during the entire day, telephone.

CH = Casa Huespedes, very simple accommodation.

CV = Club de Vacaciones. This type of accommodation is increasing in popularity: the so called "time sharing," whereby members buy a share of the accommodation for a given number of weeks during a year. This is only for club members.

F = Fonda. This is the least expensive type of accommodations for those who do not have high expectations in terms of comfort.

H = Hotels and Guest Houses are subdivided into categories depending on the number of stars (*):

A coastal panorama: the turquoise waters north of Agaete

* Heating, lift in buildings with over four floors, shower or sink in every fourth room, a bath shared by at most seven rooms, telephone on each floor, laundry service possible.

** Lift in buildings with more than three floors, reception area, bar, private bath in every eighth room, shower, sink toilet available in every second room. Telephone in every room.

*** Heating, lift, reception area, bar, complete bath in every second room. telephone in every room.

**** Air conditioning in every room and bedroom, heating, lift, at least two reception areas, bar, equipped with a parking garage in cities, the majority of rooms include a private bath, in others, usually a toilet and sink. Telephone in every room.

***** Air conditioning in every room, central heating, at least two lifts, several reception areas, laundry service possible, telephone in every room, bar, parking garage, salon on the premises.

HR = Hotel Residencia. A hotel which does not offer full board.

HS = Hostal. Guest house which almost meets the standards of a hotel but is offered at a more reasonable price.

HSR = Hostal-Residencia. Guest house which does not serve lunch or dinner.

P = Pension. Usually includes a restaurant, but does not need to purchase full board. For accommodation — whether hotel, apartment in the lower categories — one must plan on spending £5 ($9) to £10 ($18) per day. It is only rare that one will find accommodation for under £3.50 ($6).

Youth Hostels. There are two youth hostels on Gran Canaria. In →*Guia,* the hostel is open all year. In Arinaga, Tel: 75 07 86, the hostel is only open during July and August; otherwise it serves as a boarding house. Call in advance! Campsites can only be found on the island of Gran Canaria (→*Camping).* For further information on accommodation →*individual entries.*

Gran Canaria / Accommodation

Most visitors to Gran Canaria book their accommodation as part of a package tour. This is the most convenient method to secure accommodation on the island. It is also possible to look for accommodation on one's own. The least expensive options are in Las Palmas (→*Las Palmas).* Those who are less attracted to a big city can try the smaller towns of Mogan and the neighbouring town of Puerto de Mogan. The guest houses are usually run by local families, charging reasonable prices. On Gran Canaria, there are — an exception for the Canary Islands — three official campsites. Together, they can accommodate 2,000 people in tents or camping vehicles and are located in Tauro, on Temisas and in Pasito Blanco.

For further information →*individual entries.*

Agaete

Agaete is located southwest of Galdar and is accessible via road number 810. Agaete is less popular with tourists than the nearby Puerto de las Nieves with the famous Dedo de Dios.

To nurture the renowned of this city, the Captain General Señor Don Francisco Garcia-Escamez Iniesta instigated the construction of the Colegio Nacional José Sanchez y Sanchez. "For the economic use of this valley" is the wording on the commemorative plaque on this high school on Juan de Armas Street.

Living in the tidy houses — a sign of the prosperity of this town's residents — are almost 3,000 people. There are numerous stores and bar-restaurants. The chapel near the municipal park was named after the sculptor Alonso Lujan, who has produced a large proportion of the sculptures in the churches of Gran Canaria.

If one drives from Agaete farther toward Galdar, then to the right of road 810 beyond kilometre marker 32, one will come upon the cave *Cueva de las Cruces.* Strictly speaking, this is an overwhelming network of caves dug into the volcanic rock. The columns left standing support the natural ceiling. The number of Guanches who have lived here over the years can no longer be determined. However, it is certain that their livelihood was based on agriculture and animal husbandry. The fertile Valle de Agaete (there are road signs when coming from the Calle de Concepcion in Agaete) leads past San Pedro into the higher altitudes. Growing here are bananas, oranges, lemons, almonds and even coffee bushes, cocoa, avocado, mango and papaya trees.

Agaete is, however, the agricultural centre, located at the end of this fertile valley, which begins at the Berrazales Springs above San Pedro. Even in earlier times, the Guanches could appreciate this region of Gran Canaria. They lived in caves situated between Agaete and Galdar.

Accommodation: →*San Pedro, Hotel "Princesa Guayarmina."*

Casa "La Paloma," Tel: 89 81 66, near the church, £13.50 ($23.50) for two persons. The owner also rents out apartments, £19 ($33.50), across from the bank "Caja Insular" in the restaurant "Nando."

Post Office: Calle Leon y Castillo.

Taxi Stand: Calle Leon y Castillo.

Agüimes

Agüimes is often said to be a piece of the Orient on the Canary Islands. This is exaggerated. However, it is a town of radiant white with cubic houses and narrow alleyways. The San Sebastian Church in the centre of town is similar to a mosque. It houses a statue of Mary very much worth seeing: the Nuestra Señora de la Esperanza sculpted by Lujan Perez, one of the most significant foreign artists of the 15th century.

To the right of the church, a small street leads to the renowned "Barranco Guayadeque." This valley leads past a bubbling stream through a lush, fertile landscape. Caves can also be visited here. There are bars in two of these caves located directly along the road, about 4 kilometres (2½ miles) from town on the left-hand side.

The street ends after about 10 kilometres (6 miles) near a café, which charges exorbitant prices. However, this Barranco is still worth visiting. Agüimes was originally a present from the Spanish king to Bishop Juan de Frias, who provided dedicated service during the conquest of the island (→*History*). Agüimes remained the feudal seat of the Catholic bishop up until the 19th century.

Airport

The airport on Gran Canaria is called Gando and is one of the busiest airports in Spain. Almost two million tourists check in and out at the ticket counters

One of the attractions in the Agüimes Canyon: caves which still serve as housing

in Gando. Still Spain has managed to organise the air traffic so that travellers are quickly processed and the relaxation of a holiday is not abruptly ended at the airport upon embarking on the return trip. Furthermore, the airport is being expanded.

Those travelling by package tour will usually be picked up by buses belonging to or rented by the tour organisations and will be dropped off at their hotel, apartment or bungalow complex. Those travelling on their own initiative can either take a taxi or rent a car, which can be returned later or at an affiliate office after checking into one's hotel.

Car Rental

Hertz, Tel: 26 45 76 and 26 39 33.

Cicar, Tel: 70 01 65.

Occa, Tel: 70 01 66.

Avis, Tel: 70 01 57.

Aldea de San Nicolas →*Puerto de las Nieves*

Near Agüimes: dry grasses are collected everywhere for the livestock

Animals and Wildlife

There are 30 to 40 thousand cattle living on the Canary Islands, usually kept in stables and fed banana plants. Then there are the sheep and, in addition to some dromedaries and camels, there are only goats, goats and more goats. The latter are not a blessing for this island with sparse vegetation in some regions because they eat plants and shrubs down to the roots — and this is true for just about any plant. The dromedaries and camels limit their diet to thorny bushes and halophyte shrubs.

The rabbits also present a threat; however, they are also threatened: on the Canary Islands, around 50,000 hunting licences are granted annually. For every one square kilometre there are at least four hunters.

There are no snakes or scorpions on Gran Canaria, but there are lizards (Lacertas), especially geckos. The largest lizards (Lacerta simonyi) on Gran Canaria can grow up to 80 centimetres (27 inches) in length. A special species of reptile are the skinks which are often mistaken for snakes because of their slender bodies and the fact that they are sometimes legless. These are harmless and interesting to watch. Lizards, doves, ravens, thrushes and ants make themselves ecologically useful, spreading the seeds of tomatoes, grapes, laurel trees and dragon trees.

Dogs, cats and donkeys are among the most common domestic animals on the Canary Islands. The Canary bird can also be counted among these. The talkative species was in fact named after these islands.

Arguineguin

The resort town of Arguineguin, located between Maspalomas and Puerto Rico is only one bay beyond El Pajar with its cement factory. Arguineguin is predominantly a tourist centre.

Accommodation

Apartments "Aquamarina" (three keys), Patalavaca Mogan, Tel: 73 51 25. 60 apartments, between £75/$133 (for two persons) and £112/$197 (for four persons). Apartments "Montemarina" (three keys), Patalavaca Mogan, Tel: 73 52 00. Twelve apartments costing £67 ($118) for two people. Apartments "Panorama" (one key), Montaña Alta Cornisa Sur, Tel: 73 53 38. 33 Apartments, spacious enough for two or three persons, between £20 ($35.50) and £27 ($47).

Artenara

The highest village on Gran Canaria, situated at an altitude of 1,200 metres (3,960 feet) can be reached via the mountain pass GC 110 west of Cruz de

Tejeda. Artenara is a picturesque town at the upper end of an eroded canyon. At first glance, Artenara is almost reminiscent of an alpine village. A large proportion of the residents, however, live in caves carved from the volcanic rock. This is by no means an example of low-income housing. These houses are stylish abodes, built using the available materials and taking advantage of the local conditions. The sacred Virgen de la Cuevita, the virgin of the caves, is a chapel with a steeple towering over the nave. Both church and steeple were built from volcanic rock. One of the more well known attractions in Artenara is the unusual cave restaurant Meson la Silla ("Chair House"). A tunnel leads through the rock to the dining room. Beyond this, tables and the folding chairs (after which the restaurant was named) are set up as if on a huge balcony. Next to the kitchen, in which Spanish and Canarian cuisine are prepared (complete meals from £5/$9). Guests can enjoy the unparalleled view of the broad valley and the basalt boulders Roque Nublo and Roque Bentaiga. Below the cave restaurant on the opposite side of the main street, the square next to the cemetary reminds one of a Greek theatre. The square is an example of the unobtrusive landscape architecture. Various insects were sculpted into the slabs surrounding the central flower bed as a sign of respect for these small creatures.

Arucas

Arucas' wealth was a result of bananas and rum. After Las Palmas, it is the second largest city on the island with a population of 28,000 and is located halfway between Galdar and Las Palmas. Founded in 1526, Arucas appears to be full of dignity, remaining unpretentious despite its affluence, a result of the fertile valley with its banana plantations. The main point of interest is the neo-Gothic Ermita de San Pedro on the Calle Parroco Cardenes, reminiscent of the Cathedral in Cologne. It was built using volcanic rock and houses an important relic: a statue of Christ made from mahogany. The residents of Arucas like to refer to San Pedro as a cathedral. Below the church is the "Alcalde" cinema. Here, one can see a film and brush up on one's Spanish. There is also a small botanical garden in Arucas — the Parque Municipal; and in the alleyways, various restaurants with a cozy, pleasant ambience can be easily found. If one drives toward the city from the west, then one will see the "Arucas" distillery to the left after having passed the sign for "Embalses de Arucas" where bananas and rum are transformed into banana liqueur: some find this to be an acquired taste; however, one should definitely try this sweet speciality, of which the residents of Gran Canaria are so proud. Chocolate, coffee and peppermint liqueurs are also produced here. It is possible to tour the distillery (including samples!) between 8 am and 2 pm Monday to Friday. Shortly beyond the distillery, the lights of the "Howard" discotheque sparkle at night. This is one of those dance locales that is hardly different from a million other discotheques around the globe: the music is loud, the lighting dim. Devout singles comb the dance floor in search of a temporary end to their lonely existence in possibly catching an interested eye, leading then to a short trip to the Montaña de Arucas. Atop this mountain, a white neon cross stands as a reminder to young couples that Spain is a conservative Catholic country and that parents do not allow their children to do that before the wedding which is a matrimonial duty afterwards. Those who do not find the discotheque "Howard" suited to their taste can find another discotheque two kilometres outside of Arucas: the discotheque Magrodisco, along the road to Las Palmas.

On the summit of the Montaña de Arucas, a volcanic cone reaching an altitude of 512 metres, one of the most significant warriors among the Guanches stood courageously in battle against the Spaniards. Today, one can enjoy the view of the valley of Arucas, and the only battle which remains is that with the generous portions served in the restaurant "El Meson de Montaña." There are also less expensive meals: the ever-present fish, priced from £2.35 ($4.15), pickled potatoes (also called "shrunken potatoes") and Gofio, made from roasted, ground grain. Children are welcome in this restaurant, equipped with a separate play room.

Arucas / **Practical Information**

Medical Care: Pediatrician Dr. J. L. Rodriguez and Centro Medico, Leon y Castillo 4-1, Tel: 60 43 38.

Pharmacy: Calle Leon y Castillo, a total of five in Arucas.

Police: Tel: 60 40 54/8

For emergencies: 0 92

Restaurants: Restaurant "El Meson de Montaña."

Pizzeria "Penalti" across from the Grupo Escolar Generalisimo and the Music Conservatory on Dr. Fleming Street.

Ice cream parlour "Ferrera" near the taxi stand.

Important Addresses

Post Office: Calle Seruando Blanco.

Currency Exchange: various banks on the Calle Leon y Castillo.

Iberia/Trasmediterranea: Calle Francisco Gourie;

Juan de Bethancourt.

Taxi Stand: Plaza de la Constitucion;

Calle Suarez Franchy, next to the Parque Municipal.

Atalaya →*La Atalaya*

Automobile Clubs

Real Automóvile Club de España (RACE), Madrid 3, Jose Abascal 10, Tel: (91) 4 47 32 00. RACE has branch offices in: Santa Cruz de Tenerife, Tenerife, Mendez Nuñez 28 and Avenida Anaga; Tel: 27 00 70.
Las Palmas de Gran Canaria, Gran Canaria, Galo Ponte 8.
The Touring Club de España can be contacted through the address: Santa Cruz de Tenerife, Garcia Morato 14; Tel: 27 16 69.

Bargaining

Bargaining at the marketplaces on the Canary Islands is not customary. Those who do not accept these prices should purchase groceries in the supermarkets, in which the products are excellent. It is only worthwhile to try to bargain with the prices in the tourist centres when peddlers or other salesmen demand an exorbitant price for their sunglasses for example. If a price is marked, then the decision is quite simple: to buy, or not to buy.

Beaches

Those who rave about the "legendary beaches" of Gran Canaria are usually referring to the Maspalomas area. This is a region with fine, golden sand, massive dunes and beaches all the way from La Caleta to Puerto de Mogan. Here, visitors can find a secluded spot, even during peak season — which lasts the entire year. The coast of San Agustin has beaches composed of dark sand; on the other hand, there are also rugged sections of coastline.
Getting to the beach of Güigüi requires quite a lot of effort. It is exactly for this reason that it is considered one of the last beach paradises in Europe — especially by the younger generation. Güigüi lies in the northwest of Gran Canaria.
In Las Palmas, the beach Las Canteras awaits the holiday visitor: three miles of beach and bustle.
Other that these beaches, which are the destinations of those travelling by package tours or individualists with backpacks or "big-city" tourists, there are a number of bays all along the coastline suitable for swimming. These are quite secluded, and, although nudism is not officially allowed on this conservative Catholic island (with a few exceptions), it is likely that no one would notice (→*Nudism*).

Botanical Garden

Growing in the botanical garden between the upper and lower portions of the city of Tafira are unusual specimens of Canarian flora, which have become extinct in large portions of Gran Canaria. There are, however, also plants brought over from the Azores, Madeira and the Cape Verdes. A Spanish author maintained that if Gran Canaria were a microcosm of a continent, then this park would be a botanical continent. The only botanical garden similar to this on the Canaries is the Orotava Park on Tenerife.

The botanical garden of Gran Canaria is accessible via the main road connecting Las Palmas de Gran Canaria with Santa Brigida (at the kilometre marker 7). Its name in full is "Jardin Botanico Viera y Clavijo." The park is open Monday to Friday from 10 am to noon and from 3 to 7 pm. Admission is free. If one then turns off the main road to the botanical gardens, one will first come upon the park's restaurant. From the restaurant windows, one has a good overview of the park grounds. In addition, one can also enjoy a meal with a nice view at the tables near the windows.

Buses

To supplement the information under the entry *Travel on Gran Canaria,* the main bus lines and important connections between the capital and the tourist centres are included below. Bus stops on the Canary Islands are sometimes rather difficult to recognise. As a rule, one can find them on main thoroughfares; in larger towns, near the churches and main squares. One can also usually stop buses from any point between bus stops. The destinations are posted on a sign behind the bus's front window.

Bus Terminals in Las Palmas: at Park Santa Catalina, Calle Leon y Castillo, at Plaza San Telmo and Corte del Ingles (for bus routes running north). Outside the cities, the rule of thumb for bus fares is: a taxi costs ten times the bus fare to any given destination. In Las Palmas, one will pay the equivalent of about 35p (60 cents).

The departure times quoted from Las Palmas on weekdays and are subject to change. The buses travelling back to Las Palmas on the given routes have the same numbers as buses departing from Las Palmas. Information on schedule changes is available through Las Palmas, Casa del Tourismo, Parque Santa Catalina, Tel: 27 07 90 and 27 16 00.

Las Palmas — Mogan:
5, 9 and 11:10 am; 2:05, 5:10 and 7:30 pm.
Las Palmas — Puerto Rico:
Every 30 minutes between 5 am and 9:30 pm.

Las Palmas Express Bus — Maspalomas:
Every 20 minutes between 6:30 am and 7:40 pm.
Las Palmas — Caldera de Bandama:
6, 8, 8:45, 10, and 11:45 am; 2:45, 4, 8 and 9:30 pm.
Las Palmas — Tejeda:
5 and 6:45 am; 1 and 5 pm.
Las Palmas — San Mateo:
6:30 am and then from 7:40 am to 2 pm every 30 minutes; 2:30, 3:15 pm, from
3:30 to 7 pm every 30 minutes; 8, 8:30, 9 and 10 pm.
Las Palmas — Santa Brigida:
Every 30 minutes until 9:45 pm.
Las Palmas — Arucas:
Between 8:30 and 11:30 am every 15 minutes except at 11 am; then 1:15, 1:30,
1:45, 3:30, 3:45, 4:15, 4:45, 5, 5:15, 5:30, 6, 6:15, 6:45, 7, 7:30, 8, 8:30, 9:30,
10 and 11 pm.
Las Palmas — Teror:
Every 30 minutes from 6:30 am to 8:30 pm, then 9:15 and 10 pm.
Las Palmas — Firgas:
8:30 am, 12, 4:30, 6:30 and 9 pm.
Firgas — Las Palmas:
7, 8, and 10:30 am, 3:30 and 5:30 pm.
Las Palmas — Galdar and Guia:
From 10:30 am to 1:30 pm every 30 minutes, 5:30, 6:00, 6:30, 7:30, 8:30 and
10 pm.
Las Palmas — Agaete:
From 6:30 to 10 am and 2 to 6 pm every 30 minutes; 7, 8, and 9 pm.
Agaete — Las Palmas:
Via Galdar and Guia at 5 and 7 am, 12:30 and 3 pm.

Caldera de Bandama

If one drives from Las Palmas heading southeast on Road 811 toward Santa
Brigida, the one must turn left after Tafira Alta to reach Caldera de Bandama.
The crater of Bandama is located to the right-hand side of the road, which
leads up to the 569 metre high summit Pico de Bandama. The volcano has
a diameter of over 600 metres and is 200 metres deep. At its centre, a farmer
has established his own secluded settlement — a similar setting would be
difficult to find anywhere else in the world. All that is visible of the farm are
the well-tended fields and a few cows and goats near the farmhouse. The resident or residents of this farmhouse go into the nearby villages only seldom.

Traversing the path leading out of this crater can even be difficult for transport mules and strangers are never granted entrance to this crater — cynics with a note of irony say that a police officer, who used to have traffic duty on the streets of Las Palmas has fled to this crater to escape the chaos as well as the rest of the world by changing his place of residence. The road leads further along the crater and around the summit of the Pico de Bandama and then back into the lower lying surroundings. At the sign for La Atalaya, one can turn left to the Bandama golf course. The golf course is a total of 5,679 metres (6190 yards) long with 18 holes (par 72). Located directly on the golf course is the "Hotel Golf." A double room including breakfast and use of the golf course costs £50 ($88.50). Rooms are not equipped with a telephone, but with a sauna. The director of the hotel is the Swede Ingmar Werner, who is himself a golfer. Tel: 35 33 54, Fax: 35 12 90.

Bandama is not only comprised of the crater and the Pico de Bandama, but also a village with lovely houses and a wealth of gardens, flowers and decorative shrines.

A touch of the exotic: the golf course of Bandama

Camping

On the Canary Islands, there are not many official campsites: the islands are not suited for camping. Camping is not generally prohibited, but a tent will attract attention and curiosity. There are only three official campsites on the seven islands and these are all located on Gran Canaria. One of these is equipped with showers, snack bars and electricity and is, therefore, suited to those with more discerning taste. (→*Tauro*). The second is located on the crest of a mountain, west of Agüimes and is called Temisas. In the southern part of the island is an additional four-star campsite: Camping Pasito Blanco. As one leaves the town of Maspa Cornas driving west, the road branches to the left after about 5 kilometres (3 miles) leading to the yacht harbour of Pasito Blanco. Diagonally across from the fork in the road is the road leading to the campsite reception (about 50 metres/55 yards). The campsite is equipped with a swimming pool, a supermarket, a bar and showers. Price per day: campers and caravans £2 ($3.50), water and electricity £1 ($1.80), one person £1.70 ($3); a tent must be brought along and costs 70p ($1.20) per day. One can also rent a motor home which costs £13.50 ($23.50) for four people, plus the fees for the camping space. In addition to beds and a living room, these are equipped with a kitchenette. Further information: Tel: 14 21 96. This campsite is very quietly situated and is recommended for those who would like a more exclusive camping environment.

Those who would like to merely pitch a tent somewhere must be aware of the following: it is prohibited to pitch a tent within one kilometre (0.62 miles) of the coast and within 50 metres (55 yards) of the main roads. The beaches are considered everyone's; those who plan on camping out in a tent should look for a more secluded spot where he or she is not disturbed and does not disturb anyone else. If pitching a tent on a farm or private property, one must first ask permission of the owner.

Camping vehicles can be parked on public parking areas even in the larger cities without any recourse from the Policia Municipal.

Car Rental

It is definitely worthwhile to compare prices at different car rental agencies. Those offering rental cars have already adapted to this and have price lists available — sometimes under the wipers of the car itself, which one can take along on one's search. The daily rental price depends on the total length of time that the car will be rented. For example, a Seat Marbella costs around £13 ($22.50) per day if rented for three days; from four to six days, it is £10.60 ($18.85); and if rented for 7 or more days, the price drops to £30 ($17.65). The

Panda is the least expensive vehicle available to rent, but not very comfortable for tall people. A Suzuki jeep or a land rover is more comfortable to drive, but costs over twice the price of a Panda.

Upon request, personal and comprehensive insurance is available, costing around £5 ($8.85) per day per vehicle. However, for this price, one can return to the beach quickly after a police protocol has been taken, if one should have a minor accident.

One should by all means pay attention to the following:

Does the vehicle have a spare tire and tools for changing the tire? Do the turn signals, wipers, headlights and brakes function properly? Do all of the doors close securely? One must also give one's signature that the car will not be left unlocked at any time and that the vehicle was handed over in a satisfactory condition. Therefore, one should quickly check the car in the presence of the renter and make the renter aware of any deficiencies as well as any dents and scratches in the presence of witnesses.

Cenobio de Valeron

The Cenobio de Valeron network of caves is a unique example of the Guanche architecture in the northern part of Gran Canaria. 350 individual caves above and beside each other were interconnected with a complex of corridors and stairways. The "Harimaguadas," virgin priestesses once lived here. Legends recount that these temple servants lived from a special diet to strengthen them for the birth of the largest possible number of offspring.

According to another legend, the grain reserves produced in the surrounding villages were said to have been stored here and guarded by the temple priestesses. The two version of this legend do not necessarily stand in contradiction to one another: why should the attentive virgins not have nibbled on the grain they guarded?

Coming from Galdar in the west, one must then turn right shortly beyond Guia onto the road leading to the island's central regions. The caves are located high above the road in the canyon wall. Parking is available. A stairway leads up to the caves; unfortunately, most recently it is often roped off or guarded by a watchman. The caves of Cenobio de Valeron have suffered too much from the numerous visitors in recent years. If they do happen to be open (from 10 am to 1 pm and 3 to 5 pm, closed Sunday) then admission is free of charge.

Cheques →*Money*

Children

The most common holiday accommodation on Gran Canaria — bungalows and apartments — make travelling with children much easier, although hotels welcome children as well. A local babysitter can usually be arranged through the hotel reception.

Where the beaches are not gently sloping and the water not shallow, there are usually swimming and wading pools suited to children, and sometimes even attended playgrounds. When on the beach, one should definitely be cautious of the waves when swimming with children.

Climate

The Canaries are reputed to be the "islands of eternal springtime" — at least by the tour organisations. Temperatures vary only by 7 °C (13 °F) from the hottest to the coldest months.

However, it does also rain, and snow can even be found in the mountains of La Palma and Tenerife. The beaches are, however, always only a few hours away, where one can relax in the sunshine or take a stroll through the banana plantations. When travelling in summer, there is rarely a risk of bad weather. The climate is Mediterranean/subtropical. Palms, pines, sugar cane and potatoes grow only a few miles distance from each other.

On summer days, the weather can be very hot and can also be quite muggy and humid. Those travelling to the south of the island must count on a stiff breeze or even strong winds. The arid Sahara winds, the "leventas," or the haramattes blow over the islands three to four times a year, and then for up to five days. The winds transport the fine Sahara sand. It is estimated that up to 5,000 tons of sand are carried by the "levante" to Gran Canaria during the course of one year. the temperatures during this time can climb to 45 °C (114 °F) in the interior of the island with humidity falling under 30%.

The following are the average amounts of precipitation per year:

Lanzarote: 135 mm
Fuerteventura: 147 mm
Gran Canaria: 325 mm
Tenerife: 420 mm
La Gomera: 410 mm
El Hierro: 426 mm
La Palma: 526 mm

In the Anaga mountains on Tenerife and in Tamadaba on Gran Canaria, up to 1,200 mm of rain can fall during years with more moisture. In other years, in contrast, there is little rain at all. The pine forests in the mountainous regions extract the moisture from low-hanging clouds. In these regions, the precipitation can be up to 2,500 mm in a year.

On Tenerife, La Palma and Gran Canaria, the average temperature during the winter is 15 °C (60 °F); there are 6 to 10 days during a month when there is rainfall. As a result of the close proximity to the African continent and the fact that Lanzarote and Fuerteventura have no mountains, there is very little precipitation on these islands. The southern portions of the islands are drier than in the northern regions. The areas to the east of the highlands are usually cloudier. These regions are an excellent choice for a holiday during the winter or spring months; in summer, many visitors find it unbearably hot.

Gran Canaria/Climate

The epithet "islands of eternal springtime" applies to Gran Canaria as well. Not only on Gran Canaria but on all of the islands, the average temperatures range from 17 °C to 24 °C (64 °F to 76 °F).

During most of the year, it is never too hot on Gran Canaria for most of the holiday visitors. In addition, with the exception of elevations over 1,600 metres (5,232 feet), one will not encounter snowfall. However, it does rain quite often

A dramatic show of nature: the red lava cliffs shimmer in the evening sun

between November and April. One consolation: it usually never rains for more than a few hours. Afterwards it clears up becoming warm and dry. The rain is especially welcomed from May to September, when hardly any precipitation is measured.

Thanks to the currents surrounding the Canaries, the water temperature is always pleasant, between 18 °C and 23 °C (65 °F and 74 °F).

Clothing →*Equipment*

Conduct

The golden rule is always applicable: do unto others as you would have them do unto you. The guest, even when paying for the time spent on Gran Canaria should respect his or her host. Although this should go without saying, there are always discouraging scenes, especially at the bus stops. Visitors push and shove.

In some of the more expensive hotels, it is common practice to wear a tie. Those who do as the Romans when in Rome will also wear a tie during the evening meal. When visiting a church, a tie cannot hurt either. It would be completely out of context to visit the old, beautiful churches in shorts or — God forbid — in a bikini. A bikini is appropriate for the beach or the swimming pool. Otherwise they should be left in the closet — and they certainly should not be worn in museums or stores.

Topless bathing is tolerated on most of the beaches. Bathing completely nude is possible, but only on those beaches specifically set apart for this. Those who find themselves among Canarians, whose wives and daughters are wearing a bathing suit or bikini should react appropriately and forgo baring their buttocks.

Alcohol is considered a "demon" that should be kept under control, even when it is so inexpensive in this duty-free zone. Unfortunately, some visitors take advantage of the prices; barroom brawls and street fights are the results — a loss of control that could have easily been avoided.

The Spanish police should never become the brunt of jokes, ridicule or harassment. Their patent leather hat is merely a part of the uniform. Remaining objective and factual when confronted by an official is appropriate, and one should follow their instructions. This can solve the avoidable problem of having one's holiday "officially" shortened.

→*Tipping, Nudity*

Consulates →*Embassies and Consulates*
Crime →*Embassies and Consulates, Theft, Police, Behaviour*

Cruz de Tejeda

A remarkable orientation and observation point above Pozo de las Nieves in the central mountain range of Cumbre is Cruz de Tejeda. A statue of Christ stands here; from Las Palmas, 40 kilometres into the centre of Gran Canaria. The parking area is located at *Parador Nacional de Tejeda*. From there, one can see the monolith Roque Nublo (1,803 metres; 5,895 feet) El Fraile and the holy mountain of the Guanches, Roque Bentaiga (1,404 metres; 4,590 feet). One requisite is, however, that Cruz de Tejeda is not veiled in clouds at the time. Another name for this point on the island is "tempestad petrificada," in English "petrified storm." If it should happen that the weather is cloudy, then looking around the handicrafts shops or the grocery store will have to suffice as it must for numerous tourists who view the cross from a sightseeing bus. One warning to those driving a convertible or jeep: many people rent their vehicles in the island's sunny south, in Playa del Ingles or Maspalomas, and because one can easily get the idea to explore the island in shorts or a bikini by such wonderful weather, they set off for the islands interior in the late afternoon. The is when the temperatures are the highest — in Playa del Ingles and Maspalomas, that is. This is not true for Cruz de Tejeda. There, it can be bitterly cold, foggy and wet.

Restaurant

Bar-Restaurante "Cruz de Tejeda."

Cuatro Puertas

If one drives from Ingenio through the town of Carrizal, then one will reach the southbound motorway. At the exit "Telde/Base Area" one leaves the motorway and continues on the GC 812 toward Telde. After 2 to 3 kilometres (1.25 to 2 miles), one will reach a road sign "Cuatro Puertas" and 50 metres (55 yards) beyond this, an intersection. To get to the ruins on the hill Montaña de Cuatro Puertas, one must keep left and then turn left after about 100 metres (110 yards) into the small settlement. The main road leads uphill over a continually worsening slope to the fenced-in Guanche site below the summit. The last 200 metres (220 yards) are a footpath.

Cuatro Puertas is a cave in which even the tallest visitors can comfortably stand upright. It was named after the four adjacent entrances that lead to a larger hallway on the mountainside, sheltered from the wind. There are factors which substantiate the theory that these caves were used in the burial rituals because the burial rites for deceased chiefs took place on stone platforms. Among other rites, the deceased underwent a tedious mummification process.

Cueva de las Cruces →*Agaete*

Cueva Grande

To the left of the road from San Mateo via Las Lagunetas to Cruz de Tejeda is a roadway leading down to Cueva Grande. Translated, "Cueva Grande" means "big cave." However, one will search in vain for a cave here. The road leads into the mountainous forest landscape, quickly followed by a serpentine road. On this road one will certainly hope that one's car does not suddenly bread down. The serpentine finally ends below the 1,817 metre (5,940 foot) high Roque Nublo in a small village named Ayacata.

In Cueva Grande, there are only a few houses, two of which are the restaurants "El Labrador" and "Cueva Grande." These restaurants, are never very full, unless of course it rains. The region between Cueva Grande and Atalaya is a popular recreation spot. For children, it is ideal here: they can run about and play. The fact that it is often very chilly at this altitude and that a jacket is often necessary does not hinder picnic festivities.

Cuevas del Rey

Four kilometres (2.5 miles) beyond Tejeda heading toward San Bartolome, a road sign points to the right to the massive boulder of Roque Bentaiga and to the Cuevas del Rey. One will reach the caves, bored into the steep canyon walls after about 3.5 kilometres (2.25 miles). Those who arrive here on a late spring afternoon or evening before sunset can observe the unique show of nature, as the Guanche kings might have also done. Low-hanging clouds drift over the surrounding mountains into the valley, as if a poisonous, white concoction has boiled over in some laboratory.

If one drives back on the main road to San Bartolome, then one can always take a glance at the Pico del Teide, the snow-capped, volcanic mountain on Tenerife — the highest mountain in Spain.

Cuisine

Some view it as a custom, others consider it unhealthy nutrition: on the "islands of happiness" dinner is eaten quite late in the day. The Canarians rarely eat their noonday meal before 2 pm. Dinner (the evening meal) is usually not served before 8 pm. Tourism has confused these traditions somewhat, and in the larger resort cities, visitors can eat at those times to which they are accustomed (→*Time of Day*).

A Canarian breakfast consists of a type of deep-fried dough which is dunked into coffee or tea. In the hotels, however, continental (with bread rolls, ham and cheese) as well as English breakfast (with bacon and eggs and breakfast cereals) is served.

In the restaurants, European cuisine is also served. More typically Canarian cuisine can usually be found in the more remote village pubs, called "fondas," "tascas" or simply bars. The following are examples of what one can order: Snacks like salami or cheese

paella:	sometimes quite spicy, this is steamed rice in vegetable oil with prawns, mussels, different types of fish, shrimp and chicken
potaje de veduras:	thick vegetable soup
escaldon:	a thick, pulpy soup with gofio
gofio:	a bread-like, deep-fried pastry, most tasty when served fresh or toasted.
caldo:	beef bouillon
sopa:	soup with meat or sausage

Ripening in the sunshine of Gran Canaria: mountain vineyards

gazpacho:	tomato soup
sopa de mariscos:	mussel soup
patates:	sweet potatoes
papas arrugadas:	shrunken pickled potatoes
queso blanco:	goat's cheese
vino tinto:	red wine
cuba libre:	cola with locally produced rum
sangria:	wine with fruit, also called "the liquid hangover"
cafe solo:	dark roasted coffee
cafe con leche:	coffee with milk

Culture

Those who are not particularly interested in Stone Age relics will be disappointed in what remains of the original culture of Gran Canaria: the Guanches left only mummies, skulls and pieces of pottery behind for the museums.

The peaks of the Cumbre mountain range present splendid views of the surrounding landscapes

What is noticeably better represented are remnants of the Canarian culture, documenting the development after the conquest of the islands:

The historical buildings on the Canary islands contain Gothic, Renaissance and Baroque elements. Visitors will note the similarity between the El Salvador Church in Santa Cruz de La Palma and other European cathedrals like the cathedral in Cologne. The richly embellished balconies and ceilings built from Canarian pine, are reminiscent of southern Spain.

The combination of Gothic and intricate Moorish elements in the "Mudejar" style was foremost practised by artisans and craftsmen with Arabian heritage, who were converted to the Christian faith between the 13th and 15th centuries. There horseshoe arches, ceiling and Majolika ornamentation and a wealth of geometrical designs in these forms can also be found on the Canary Islands. The plateresque style is termed as the "goldsmith" style (Spanish: "plateresco") even though the works of art are not made of metal but are carved from wood. Those who tactfully wander into the inner courtyards of the residential houses will be pleasantly surprised: the patios are lovingly decorated with plants and the stairways are especially pretty.

Cumbre

Cumbre is the central mountain range (mountain range) on Gran Canaria with Pozo de las Nieves at its centre and the Roque Nublo, a monolith towering 60 metres (195 feet).

Currency → *Money*

Customs Regulations

Upon entry there are no customs limitations in the duty-free zone of the Canary Islands. One must, however, pay attention to the Spanish customs regulations when travelling from the Canaries to the Spanish mainland.

When returning to the United Kingdom, one may being along 200 cigarettes or 50 cigars or 250 grams of tobacco as well as 1 litre of spirits and 2 litres of wine.

When returning to the United States, one may being along 200 cigarettes and 100 cigars and a reasonable amount of tobacco as well as 1 litre of spirits or 1 litre of wine.

Dedo de Dios → *Puerto de las Nieves*

Discounts

Children under 14 pay half the adult fare when using public transportation (buses and boats); children under 4 ride free. As a rule, the same is true for admission to amusement parks. If uncertain, one should definitely ask.

International car rental agencies such as InterRent, Avis and Hertz grant members of their clubs discounts of up to 25% off the normal rental price. It is, however, still worth comparing prices: an Opel Corsa or Ascona is, as a general rule, always more expensive than a Fiat Panda, which are frequently offered by local rental agencies at low prices (→Car Rental).

Distances

When planning day trips, one can easily underestimate the distances on Gran Canaria: the maps (→Maps) usually include no distances, or those included are inexact. The roads are in part such tangled serpentines that planning a trip accurately is seldom possible. The consequences of this are that one might have to spend the night in the car or in a remote hotel — given that a hotel can be found.

The "Tourism Maps of Gran Canaria" and the "Hildebrandt Distance Tables" have proven to be more accurate. These are available at the newsstands and book stores on Gran Canaria. Among others, the distances to the capital of Las Palmas are listed in these publications. A visit to the capital should definitely be included in one's holiday plans. Therefore, the distances between Las Palmas de Gran Canaria and several other towns are listed here:

Agaete 45 km (28 miles), Agüimes 37 km (23 miles), Artenara 52 km (33 miles), Arucas 17 km (11 miles), Guia 30 km (19 miles), Playa del Ingles 52 km (33 miles), Maspalomas 53 km (34 miles), Puerto de Mogan 88 km (55 miles), Puerto Rico 71 km (45 miles), San Agustin 49 km (31 miles), San Bartolome de Tirajana 63 km (40 miles), San Nicolas de Tolentino 82 km (52 miles), Tasarte 98 km (62 miles), Tejeda 42 km (27 miles), Telde 17 km (11 miles), Teror 21 km (14 miles), San Mateo 22 km (14 miles).

Economy

The most important branches of the economy are, in addition to tourism, agriculture and the fishing industry. In historical times, the pigments of Orchilla and Orseille (Rocella tinctoria) used in the production of purple dyes played a significant economical role on the eastern Canary Islands (→History). In the 19th century, the opuntias were introduced, and with them, the cocheneal, a louse, whose purple pigment "Carmine" is still used in the production of lipstick which later colours the lips red (→Vegetation).

Fishing (especially anchovies and tuna) is concentrated between Fuerteventura, Lanzarote and the African continent. These waters are also fished by a large proportion of foreign fishing fleets. The Canarians fish mainly to cover domestic demand.

The harbours of Las Palmas and Tenerife continue to gain importance. In Santa Cruz de Tenerife, there is even an oil refinery.

Canarian cigars are produced in small tobacco factories in Las Palmas de Gran Canaria, Santa Cruz de Tenerife and Santa Cruz de La Palma, which can compete with their counterparts from Havana.

In 1974, 400,000 metric tons of bananas were produced on 12,000 hectares of plantation land, of which 90% were exported to the Spanish mainland. The Canaries have the advantage that the distance to the shipping harbours is always short. This makes it possible for even sensitive fruits, like the Indonesian or Cavendish banana to reach the consumer quickly. The Canary Islands also produced 135,000 metric tons of tomatoes on an area of 7,000 hectares in 1974. These were mainly exported countries other than Spain in Western Europe. In the moist, cloudy regions in the north and central regions of Gran Canaria, potatoes are the main crop. The potato crops on the Canary Islands can be harvested twice a year. Tobacco, onions and sweet potatoes are harvested on La Palma and Lanzarote as well. Green peppers and cucumbers thrive in the greenhouses; egg-plants in the irrigated fields. Also growing in the greenhouses of the Canaries are roses, chrysanthemums and carnations as export goods. An area of 425 hectares of the islands are used in gardening. Sugar cane, which played an important role in the 18th century, has become an insignificant economical factor today. Only in the northern regions of Gran Canaria is rum produced from the sugar cane grown on this island. Grapes for the production of the excellent Canarian red and light muscatel wines are grown on Lanzarote and Gran Canaria (El Monte, in the Tafira region). Another well known wine is the malvasia, produced on Lanzarote, El Hierro and La Palma. The production of wines has, however, decreased dramatically since the 19th century when mildew destroyed a large proportion of the grape vines.

The Canary Islands are geographically fascinating. However, visitors must often hike for hours to see the points of geographical interest. Inevitably come upon the evidence of unfamiliar agricultural methods:

"Secano" is the Canarian term for the farming of an irrigated field. A special type of agricultural technique is called "enarenando," the non-irrigated method, where plants are placed in 200 to 800 shallow funnels per hectare, for example on Tenerife and especially often on Lanzarote. Then is also the method of covering the ground with grey pumice called "jable" in the sand dunes of Lanzarote. Mixing the soil with yellow pumice is termed "sahorra." The reason for this is to absorb warmth during the day, whereby the soil then quickly cools in the evening, collecting the condensation. The plants thrive as if in a greenhouse, the humus protected from the wind by pumice and earthen retaining walls.

Crops cultivated using the "enarenando" method are corn, potatoes, yams, tomatoes, tobacco, grapes, barley, oats, alfalfa, most of the fruit trees and opuntias. The "jable" method, used in the southern regions of Tenerife between Granadilla, Vilaflor and San Miguel — or on extensive tracts of land on Lanzarote — is employed in cultivating wheat, barley, tomatoes, watermelons and cucumbers.

The "sahorra" method allows for up to four harvests on the same fields per year on El Hierro: tomatoes between August and December; potatoes between December and March and again around May; corn up until August.

Gran Canaria / Economy

Meanwhile, the most important economic branch on Gran Canaria is tourism. Of course, the harbour of Puerto de la Luz in Las Palmas also plays a significant role in the economy, but it cannot compete with the 1.75 million tourists that visited Gran Canaria between January and November in 1987, for example. The neighbouring island of Lanzarote, in comparison, could record only 562,000 visitors during the same period, and Fuerteventura trails, having hosted only 279,000 tourists during this period.

El Espinillo

El Espinillo is a sleepy little village near Roque Bentaiga, seemingly untouched by modern times.

El Oasis →*Maspalomas*

El Pajar

El Pajar is not terribly popular with holiday travellers — its cement factory "Cementos Especiales S.A." is too reminiscent of the workday at home. El Pajar is located between the beach and the unpretentious holiday town of Arguineguin and Puerto Rico in the southern part of Gran Canaria. One must turn left at a confusing intersection to reach the town comprised only of the cement factory and apartment houses where the factory workers live. There are several locales that one should visit if looking for contact with the Spaniards. This is certainly not easy to find in the southern part of the island.

A very important attraction for this town is the "Knutschi," a Fiat 500 which has found its last parking place perched on a sawed-off tree stump (to the right of the road when entering town).

El Risco

Halfway between Agaete and Puerto San Nicolas, the picturesque whitewashed houses in the farming village of El Risco seem to hang on the mountain slopes. A sand roadway leads from the centre of the village down to one of the few secluded gravel beaches on the northwestern coast. One must walk the last few metres to the water because the roads are not passable by car and are, therefore, usually closed off to traffic. There are two bar/restaurants in El Risco that can be recommended for having a snack: the bars "Perdomo" and "Las Viveas." Accommodation is difficult to find in this village; the proprietors of the two bars might be able to arrange private rooms.

Electricity

The voltage on the Canary Islands varies: sometimes it is 110 to 125 volts alternating current, in the tourist centres, 220 volts. Those who do not want to forgo bringing their electric shaver or blow dryer, should take this into consideration. The appropriate sockets are also not always available. An adapter should, therefore, be brought along.

Embassies and Consulates

United States Embassy
Calle Serrano 75
Madrid, Spain
Tel: 2 76 36 00, in emergencies Tel: 2 76 32 29

Canadian Embassy
Calle Nuñez de Balboa 35
Madrid, Spain
Tel: 4 31 43 00

British Embassy
Calle Fernando el Santo 16
Madrid, Spain
Tel: 4 19 15 28

Australian Embassy
Paeso de la Castellana 143
Madrid, Spain
Tel: 2 79 85 01

Las Palmas de Gran Canaria
British Consulate
Calle Alfredo L. Jones 33
Las Palmas, Gran Canaria
Tel: 26 25 08

Emergencies →*Automobile Clubs, Police, Medical Care*

Entertainment

The Canary Islands have everything from discotheques to night clubs and even sports facilities and guided tours and excursions — everything that will augment an enjoyable holiday. To avoid misunderstandings, here are a few general remarks:

A "restaurante" is a restaurant. A "bar" is not necessarily a night club but a café, a snack bar, or a wine bar serving wine directly from the barrel.

The atmosphere in night clubs and discotheques first picks up around midnight. Folklore and singing groups usually do not begin their performances until 11 pm — but then they last until around 3 am. The Canarian music has Andalusian and South American elements. The "islas" are ironic; the "folias," emotional; the "arroros," sentimental; and the "canarios" are lively, vibrant songs. the latter are so popular that even Louis XIV had them performed in his court.

Both the provincial capitals of Las Palmas de Gran Canaria and Santa Cruz de Tenerife have theatres. The Teatro de Guimera in Santa Cruz de Tenerife (Calle Imeldo Seris), as well as the Teatro Perez Galdos (Calle Triana) in Las Palmas, are the most widely known, in which predominantly operas are performed.

Equipment

On the islands of "eternal springtime," one must be prepared for any type of spring weather: during the day, it can get quite warm (→*Climate);* at night, in contrast, it can get so cool that a sweater should not be missing from anyone's luggage. Trips to the neighbouring islands of La Palma, La Gomera, El Hierro, Tenerife and Fuerteventura lead through damp and cold areas, especially when it is foggy and windy. Along the coasts and when swimming, it is appropriate to wear light tennis shoes or plastic sandals because the way to the beach is often over sharp stones or gravel.

Because the sun can become very intense, a hat and (for those with sensitive eyes) sunglasses are recommended in addition to the usual bathing equipment. For those wishing to camp on Gran Canaria: a light aluminium sleeping bag indeed takes up little space; however, it is unsuited for the relatively chilly nights on the Canary Islands. A down sleeping bag is more appropriate.

Excursions to Neighbouring Islands

Three excursions are especially worthwhile: Fuerteventura is the island directly to the east; north of Fuerteventura is Lanzarote. Both islands belong to the province of Las Palmas de Gran Canaria. Thirdly, Tenerife, the largest neighbour to the east with the volcanic mountain Pico del Teide as its trademark, is the main island in the province of Santa Cruz de Tenerife, which also includes the islands of El Hierro, La Gomera and La Palma.

Fuerteventura

Fuerteventura's *Puerto del Rosario* is accessible by ship from Las Palmas. In addition, there are daily flights from the Gando airport to Fuerteventura (→*Travel on Gran Canaria*). Fuerteventura is an island which some find to be a paradise; others think it a type of hell "that only tourists can withstand — and tourists seem to go everywhere. That which was built here in the past few years to attract the thousands of tourists is no different from that which can be seen in any other tourist centre." And still: there are reasons for which this island is incomparable and worth visiting, for instance, the old defence tower near *Castillo de Fuste* in the eastern portion of the island south of the capital. The foundations were already laid many years prior to the recent opening of the restaurant located within. The yacht harbour is quite definitely worth the trip.

A beautiful village with old structures, *Corralejo* is in the northern part of the island. And, due to the fact that there are simply not many older things to market on Fuerteventura, Corralejo has to suffer the consequences: apartment complexes, hotels and standard tourist bars and discotheques have been built up all around this town.

The capital of Puerto del Rosario is deemed "interesting" by benevolent authors with a good portion of distance. The city is young, fulfils the expectations placed on a capital city as an administration centre. Those who stay here for a longer period of time are either tourists who missed their boat leaving from the harbour or they are members of the foreign legion. The latter are everywhere — not by choice. An order is, after all, an order.

Remaining to be mentioned is *Betancuria,* the old capital of the island — a jewel from the 15th century in a secluded valley. This city can be recommended for a visit without reservation, especially because of that which has endured over the centuries. If not the man-made attractions, then it is the fascinating landscapes that will draw interest: the beaches on the western and eastern coast and the sand dunes near Corralejo which are similar to those near Maspalomas on Gran Canaria. Precisely this is emphasised in the travel brochures. Sand from the Sahara was blown over from Africa to land on the eastern coast of Fuerteventura, a swimming area which is truly deserving of the superlative. The Golfo region on the *Jandia* peninsula with its mountains is another of Fuerteventura's assets. From the top of one of the dunes, one has a breathtaking view of the beach, stretching for miles in the western part of Jandia. The attraction does, however, diminish somewhat: these beaches are only conditionally suited for swimming due to the rough seas.

Fuerteventura is the second largest island of the Canaries, but still has a population of only a little over 20,000. The reasons for this are the arid climate and lack of water which place high demands on the residents. The fact that all of this was placed in a positive light in the tourist areas over the past 20 years is understandable: Fuerteventura was once suited as an exile colony. However, the island has its attractive sides — which almost any wind surfer will gladly confirm.

Lanzarote

Lanzarote can be reached by ship from Las Palmas via Fuerteventura or directly by airplane from Gando airport in the shortest amount of time *(→ Travel on Gran Canaria).* Lanzarote is a volcanic island, making it worth seeing solely for this reason. Those wanting to experience the unusual sides of nature will find themselves continually amazed at what this island has to offer. Lanzarote is, however, so small that the sights it has to offer which are the greatest distance from each other can be reached in one and a half to two hours. Not far from Playa Blanca on the southern tip of Lanzarote are *El Golfo,* the rugged coast of *Los Hervideros* and the *Salinas of Janubio,* which one should definitely see, even when one is not at first terribly impressed with the strictly geometrical shapes of the salt basins. El Golfo is renowned for its huge crater in the shaped of a half moon and filled with water with a high salt concentration. A barrier made of sand protects this natural swimming pool from drying up. Sea water continually seeps inland, but the impression of a "dead sea" remains. The lake is named Lago Verde because of its green shimmer. One can stroll or go for a swim along the long, black sandy beaches. Other than directly along the crater, the coast of El Golfo is rugged and windy. The craggy coast of Los Hervideros is located between the Salinas of Janubio and El Golfo on the western coast of Lanzarote. This infertile land is characterised by sharp-edged, petrified lava. Los Hervideros is a destination for numerous tourists buses, but also for individual travellers as well. Amid the barren landscape — only green lichen grow in the volcanic ash — the surf has deepened the crevices in the lava, creating a type of labyrinth. The waves pound the coast, frothing and foaming. "Hervideros" is the Spanish word for gushing or churning. "Olivina" is sold along the coast of Los Hervideros. This light green semi-precious volcanic stone is called "peridot" by mineralogists. Its colour results from magnesium and iron silicates which were formed millions of years ago. There are only a few volcanic islands where Olivina can be found. One of these is Lanzarote, from which Olivina is also exported to Tenerife. The demand for this stone was always high since it is similar to emerald in appearance. Owing to this, it was used not only during the baroque period as a stone in jewellry but also in the ornamentation of churches. The Salinas de Janubio are situated to the left of the main road when driving north from Playa Blanca. They shimmer white and pink in the sunshine. Continuing north, one will come to *La Geria,* the main area used in the cultivation of the delicious wine of Lanzarote. This region conveys an impression of the hard work needed to raise crops of grapes from the dry soil. The landscape of La Geria, between Arrecife, the capital of Lanzarote and the Montañas del Fuego, is characteristic of Lanzarote. After the volcanic eruptions in the 18th and 19th centuries, a third of the island was covered by a blanket of lava. Resulting from these volcanoes were the geologically unique *Timanfaya National Park* with its *Montañas del Fuego,* the mountains of fire. These mountains form a bizarre landscape in the island's southwestern highlands. Most of these volcanoes were formed during the eruptions from 1730 to 1736. During this time, a quarter of Lanzarote's surface of 200 square kilometres was covered by lava and volcanic ash. The epicentre of volcanic activity focussed around the Timanfaya, another term for the Montañas del Fuego. The trip then continues further northwards by a monument in honour of the hard work of Lanzarote's farmers: the *Monumento al Campesino.* This monument was erected between Mozaga and San Bartolome at the centre of Lanzarote by the artist and architect Cesar Manrique and his team. Directly next to this is a simple yet harmonically conceived farmhouse which is a good example of the architecture of Lanzarote. Farming equipment was also set up here and there is a restaurant/bar with food typical of the Canary Islands as well as the malvasia wine, native to this island. A ceramics exhibition displays works by the artist Juan Jesus Brito, who made a portrait of the

Canarian royal family based on historical documentation. A further sight, also created by Cesar Manrique is the lookout point *Mirador del Rio,* which is accessible via a well paved road in the northern portion of Lanzarote. The lookout point, high above the strait between the island of Graciosa and Lanzarote's northern coast, is a work of art, reminiscent of the residents' original domiciles in caves. Hidden behind the facade is a spacious two-story structure with tastefully decorated hallways, elegantly sweeping stairways and foyers. If one remains on the road in the southeastern portion of the island, one will come upon a natural wonder comparable to the Montañas del Fuego: the volcanic grottoes *Jameos del Agua* and *Cueva de los Verdes.* Jameos del Agua is the largest volcanic grotto in the world and is interconnected with Cueva de los Verdes. Both are located near the coast in Lanzarote's northeast. The underground cave, Cueva de los Verdes in the lava fields of Malpaises de Corona north of Arrieta and near Jameos del Agua served as a hideout for the original inhabitants of Lanzarote. On the one hand, they hid from the Spaniards; on the other, from pirates who invaded the island from Europe or Africa.

Tenerife

Tenerife can be reached by ship from Puerto de la Luz in Las Palmas or by airplane from the Gando airport *(→Travel on Gran Canaria).* One should plan several days for a trip to this island. Above all, the flower gardens and canyons, the snow-covered peak of *Pico del Teide,* desert landscapes, lava cliffs, Guanche caves and skyscrapers. *Loro Parque* with its numerous species of parrots near Puerto de la Cruz and the *Octopus Aguapark* near Playa del Ingles count among Tenerife's attractions. An extraordinary landscape for swimming is the artificial *Lago Martianez* in Puerto de la Cruz — and *Santa Cruz* is an amiable capital city. Those who travel to Tenerife by ship will arrive in the harbour of Santa Cruz. Annually, over 10,000 transatlantic ships, freight ships, fishing boats and banana steamers dock in this harbour as well as the largest proportion of ships operating between the islands. With a population of 191,000, almost half of the total population of Tenerife lives in the capital. The city is bisected by Barranco de Santos: the northern portion is modern; the southern portion is poorer and older and also partially an industrial area. Directly on the harbour, which is integrated into the city, stands the famous memorial to the fallen soldiers in the Spanish Civil War (1936-1939) located at the end of the elegant coastal road Avenida de Anaga in the centre of the Plaza de España. One can find the *Archaeological Museum* directly at the beginning of the Avenida Bravo Murillo, which begins at Plaza de España. It is open daily from 9 am to 1 pm and 4 to 6 pm. Adults pay £1 ($1.75);

admission is free of charge for children and students. Further sights in Santa Cruz de Tenerife:

- the central market *Mercado de Nuestra Señora de Africa* with the oriental clock tower.

- the *Plaza de Weyler* with the fish in the lovely marble fountain and the palace of the Captain Generals in which General Franco also lived up until July 16, 1936, before he declared the Spanish Civil War and set off for the Spanish mainland.

- the *Parque Garcia Sanabria* with its numerous flower beds, cafés, children's playgrounds and a miniature golf course; it carries the name of one of the governors and significant benefactor of the city.

- the *Municipal Museum of Fine Arts,* in which, however, old weapons will compete with the sculptures and paintings for the visitor's attention.

- the oldest church of Santa Cruz de Tenerife, the *Iglesia de la Concepcion* (1502). Inside this church, one can view memorabilia from the time of the conqueror Alonso Fernandez de Lugo and the flags of Lord Nelson, defeated in 1797.

The suggestion not missing from any travel guide: the dragon tree of *Icod de los Vinos,* which can be admired during a tour of the city. However, there are many other "dragos" in addition to this; the oldest is estimated to be a thousand years old. One example where more can be found is in the university city of La Laguna.

Faro de Sardina →*Sardina*

Fataga

In the southern portion of the island, a winding road leads 23 kilometres (15 miles) from San Bartolome directly to the dunes of Maspalomas. Only 5 km (about 2½ miles) beyond San Bartolome is the wealthy village of Fataga with its whitewashed houses and pretty gardens. In the early morning hours, the residents are already underway to Maspalomas where they earn their living in the hotels and restaurants.

The cornerstone for the church was laid on June 18, 1880. One hundred years later, a memorial plaque was added in honour of the village residents who helped in its construction.

Across from the church, wooden articles, baskets and textile handicrafts are sold. These are also sold in the tourist centres but at a much higher price than in Fataga.

Fataga is situated near the canyon Barranco de Fataga, in which the spurge plants, shaped like candelabras have put down roots *(→ Vegetation)*. The reservoir Presa de Fataga lies to the right of the road leading to Maspalomas. It has however dried up.

Accommodation: Private accommodation possible; take note of signs posted.
Restaurants and Bars: Bar-Restaurante "Labrador" and "Perez" Bar (near the souvenir shop); both on Calle de Nestor Alamo.
Restaurante "Esmeralda," 3 km (2 miles) beyond the southern exit from town on the left-hand side; includes a small bird park.
Service Station: Before the southern exit from town on the left-hand side.

Ferries *→Travelling to Gran Canaria, Travel on Gran Canaria*

Firgas

Every holiday traveller on Gran Canaria and the neighbouring islands is familiar with Firgas because of the drinking water "Aguas de Firgas," which is bottled in plastic containers and canisters 7 kilometres (4½ miles) south of Maya.

Nestled in a green oasis: the mountain village of Fataga

One can drive through Firgas on the road GC 814 coming from Arucas in the north and heading toward Teror, a site of pilgrimage in the southern part of the island.

Other than its role of supplying drinking water for the Canaries, Firgas is less interesting. Worth mentioning is the "Las Madres" spa, which is also fed from the natural springs of Firgas.

Folklore

The painter Nestor de la Torre (in whose honour the Museo Nestor in Las Palmas de Gran Canaria was built) designed colourful costumes according to old, almost forgotten patterns at the beginning of the 20th century. These costumes are still worn on all of the Canary Islands as folklore costumes during "Canarian Evenings" and festivals.

These evenings are organised by almost every tour organisation or one can inquire at the travel agencies in the tourist centres or in larger hotels.

The songs play the most prominent role in these performances. Love is the most popular theme which is presented sometimes ironically, sometimes romantically. The lyrics are accompanied by the small "timple" similar to a guitar and typical for Canarian music.

According to the legends handed down on the Canary Islands, the Guanches and Spaniards made less of a historical and literary mark than did the Greeks. The Greek sagas claim that the Canary Islands are the remains of the sunken city of Atlantis. According to another story, the gardens of Hesperides were found on these islands — gardens where the apples of eternal youth could be found. When considering that apples do not grow here and that the Canary Islands have a number of beautiful cemeteries, this legend must remain a legend.

Although people still do find their final resting place on these islands, they make the most of life up until this time. This is reflected by the saying "Salud, amor y dinero — y el tiempo para gozarlo," meaning "health, love and money — and time enough to enjoy it all." And part of enjoying life is eating well. A staple is "Gofio" *(→Cuisine)*, of which the men claim: Gofio gives us the energy that women take.

Fontanales

Finding Fontanales on a map is no easy task; on some "San Bartolome" is written in its place, which should not be confused with San Bartolome de Tirajana located much further to the south. Fontanales can be reached via the winding road GC 160 after about 14 kilometres (9 miles). Beyond the entrance

to the city on the throughway are the restaurants "Silbora" and "Fontanales."
In Fontanales, one can visit two churches. The more beautiful of the two is
also the larger, located on Calle Fleming. The front portion was constructed
later than the back portion. Not far away is the second church named after
Fontanales and with which the towns history began. From here in the mountains, one can sometimes observe the shearing of sheep (cortigo de pavon).
This is a performance in and of itself, in which the entire village takes part.
Afterwards, there is a celebration with wine and music. This festival is, however,
not a tourist attraction. Usually, only the residents take part in the festivities,
but individual visitors who have spoken with Pepe Mendosa beforehand are
welcome. It is best to ask for him in the two restaurants.

Foreign Currencies →*Money*
Fuel →*Travel on Gran Canaria*

Fuente de los Azulejos

Western Gran Canaria is an area filled with springs and reservoirs (fuentes
and embalses). The Fuente de los Azulejos is located between Mogan and
San Nicolas de Tolentino. What characterises this spring, however, is a greenish
blue shimmering rock directly on the road shortly before the turn-off to Tasarte,
when approaching from Mogan. A fruit and refreshment stand offers the chance
for an inviting break with its small parking area as well as covered picnic
benches.

Galdar

The banana-growing region of Galdar, which is also the largest city in the northwestern portion of Gran Canaria at the foot of the Montañas de Galdar, has
a population of 4,000; when the surrounding regions are included, 16,000.
Galdar is only about 30 kilometres (19 miles) from Las Palmas and is accessible via the road GC 810.
Earlier, Galdar was the governmental seat of the Guanche Princes, the
Guanarteme. This is also where the conquest of Gran Canaria ended in 1483.
The last opponent, the Guanarteme Tenesor Semidan was overpowered, converted to Christianity and baptised Fernando de Guanarteme.
Today, Galdar is a bustling, noisy city. Despite the grey and the dust that is
churned up by the traffic from the surrounding regions and tourist centres,
it is still a pretty city, definitely worth mentioning.
In the centre of this town, at the end of Calle Capitan Queseda, on can escape
the noise of the main street on the shady Plaza de Santiago. The Santiago

Church was first built in place of the old Guanarteme Palace in the 18th century to serve as a reminder that the new rulers had also brought a new belief with them. Inside, one can see various statues of the resurrection, the Virgin of the Roses and a green ceramic baptismal font. They were mane by Lujan Perez, who was brought to the island from Andalusia. Perez converted and baptised many Canarians into Christian faith.

Galdar / **Practical Information**

Currency Exchange: Approximately 10 different banking institutions.
Dental Care: Clinica Dental on the Drago Road toward Las Palmas.
Iberia: Calle Capitan Queseda.
Post Office: on Plaza los Faicanes.
Police: Calle Aljirofe.
Shopping: The best area for shopping is in the market centre on the main shopping street Capitan Queseda.

Gando →*Airport*

Geography

Many islands, many worlds — highly appropriate to the Canary Islands. Tenerife was once called the "flower island," although this was linguistic plagiarism: "Flora" is the name of an island in the Azores with a large amount of precipitation, dense vegetation and the profuse flowers which give the island its name. However, neither Tenerife nor Gran Canaria pale in comparison. Due to their climatic zones and geography, Domingo Cardenes even called the latter "continente en miniature" — a continent in miniature.

The Canary Islands are located between 27° 37° (Punta Restinga on El Hierro) and 29° 23° (Aleganza Island) northern latitude and 13° 20° (Roque del Este) and 18° 16° (Punta Orchilla on El Hierro) western longitude in the region of northwestern Africa.

Owing to this location in the Atlantic, the wind is never perfectly calm: either the hamatte winds blow over from the African continent in the east or the tradewinds from over the Atlantic in the west.

This archipelagos lies at the same latitude as the sunny paradise of Florida or Egypt. It can also get quite dry here: the irrigated arable land on the Canary Islands is estimated at about 3 to 6% of the total surface, 18% for non-irrigated

Simultaneously fascinating and desolate: the rugged canyons carved into the volcanic landscape ▶

farming. 44% is pastureland or forests; the rest of the area is unproductive. The Canary Islands extend over 500 kilometres (315 miles) from east to west. The shortest distance to the African continent — a little over 100 kilometres (63 miles) — is measured from Cape Juby on Fuerteventura. The islands are 1,100 kilometres (692 miles) from Gibraltar and about 4,000 kilometres (2,516 miles) from Central Europe.

Reports as to the exact size of the Canary Islands differ, varying up to 700 square kilometres (270 square miles). The Consejo Economico Social Sindical de Canarias (CESSCAN) calculated the area of all islands from Lanzarote (Alegranza) at the northeastern tip to El Hierro, the southwestern most extreme at 7,466 square kilometres (2,883 square miles) in 1973.

With only 80 kilometres (50 miles) of ocean separating them, Tenerife and Gran Canaria make up the centre of the archipelagos. La Gomera, El Hierro and La Palma surround these two main islands. La Gomera is only 23 kilometres (15 miles) from Tenerife, 60 to 65 kilometres (38 to 42 miles) separate the three western islands.

The flat eastern islands of Lanzarote and Fuerteventura make a geographical unit. They are 85 kilometres (54 miles) from Gran Canaria and run almost parallel to the African Coast. Their direct neighbours are the isletas: located between Fuerteventura and Lanzarote is Losbos; north of Lanzarote are Graciosa, Alegranza, Montaña Clara, Roque del Este and Roque del Oeste. These islands are not all inhabited, but some do in part serve as pastureland. Lanzarote and Fuerteventura are also called the "purple islands" because a lichen used in the production of purple dyes was found here. The islands to the west are distinguished from the others by the term "Fortunatas" from the Latin "insulae fortunatae" meaning "islands of good fortune." The vegetation is described as macronesic, which comes from the Greek meaning no more than "the flora of the islands of good fortune."

The eastern islands are on Africa's continental shelf, the others were formed by volcanic activity without being on the continental shelf. With this, the hypothesis that the Canary Islands were the remnants of the legendary sunken city of Atlantis was disproved. The western islands have nothing in common, geographically speaking.

All of the islands have three factors in common: the eroding action of flowing water, the abrasive activity of the ocean's surf and, above all, volcanism. This is how the slopes consisting of blankets of lava in varying thickness were formed. These are composed of volcanic rock, black basalt, acidic lava like andesite and trachyte, light pumice and old, charred soil — the bright red "almagre." Sometimes, one can find caves in the canyon walls or walls of basalt and phonolyte on the islands, the most significant characteristic of which is the columnar structure.

The world of volcanic formations is characterised mainly by two shapes. The linear volcano, formed by a chain of volcanic activity and the conic or cauldron volcano. The former is a type of volcano which built up along a crevice — a chain of smaller volcanoes. This type of volcano makes clear that the Canary Islands, like the Azores, belong to a fault system cutting through the mid-Atlantic ridge from east-southeast to west-northwest. The most common volcanic formation on the Canary Islands is without question the "caldera" volcano, a type of cauldron crater that presumably originates from the explosion or collapse of the original volcanic cone. A lake is commonly found at the base of this type of crater.

The Canary Islands are presumed to have been formed around 20 million years ago, whereby the eastern islands of Fuerteventura and Lanzarote are possibly even older. Found here were the fossilised eggs of prehistoric land bird also capable of flight and similar to an ostrich. The Canary Islands are at least closely related to the African continent and the theory that they were connected to the continent by a land bridge cannot be disproven. Fossilised bones of a giant lizard were also found on Tenerife. Fossilised impressions of plant life like pines and laurel stems on Gran Canaria and Tenerife are dated at 600,000 years. Lanzarote, Tenerife and La Palma were still sights of volcanic activity in recorded history. On Gran Canaria, Fuerteventura and possibly on El Hierro, eruptions could have occurred in the late prehistoric era. On La Gomera, eruptions occurred up to the start of the Quarternary Period.

The following eruptions have been documented:

1393 and 1399
1430
1484
1492 (reported in Christopher Columbus' logbook)
1604 Siete Fuentes Volcano
1605 Fasnia Volcano
1704 Güimar Volcano
1705 Güimar Volcano
1706 Garachico Volcano
1798 Chahorra Volcano
1909 Chinyero Volcano

La Palma:
1585 Volcano del los Llanos
1677 Tigalate Volcano

1677 Fuencaliente Volcano
1705 or 1725 Volcano del Charco
1949 Volcano de las Manchas

Lanzarote:
1824 Tao Volcano, Nueva de Fuego and Tinguation.

Gran Canaria / Geography

The island has an area of 1,532 square kilometres (592 square miles), is 47 kilometres (30 miles) in width and 55 kilometres (34 miles) in length. It lies 1,000 kilometres (630 miles) south of the Spanish mainland and 350 kilometres (220 miles) west of Africa. Gran Canaria is almost perfectly round with the Pozo las Nieves measuring 1,949 metres (6,373 feet) in height at its centre. The Pozo de las Nieves, which translates as "well" or "depression of snow," is the highest peak in the central mountain range with its beautiful pine forests of Tamadaba (Pinar de Tamadaba). Gran Canaria looks like one huge volcanic cone protruding from the ocean, with the Isleta connected to its northern coast

In the interior of the volcanic island, the barren landscape is punctuated by bizarre rock formations

by the Isthmus of Guanarteme. The island is severed by the network of valleys on all sides of the volcanic slopes. The massive canyons Barrancos de Tejeda and de Tirajana border on the highlands. The southern portions, the Tamaran, leads steeply up to a high plateau. Gran Canaria is formed like a "shield volcano," categorised by geologists as the Hawaiian type. The radial epicentre of eruption lay in the western part of the island. Fertile plains can be found predominantly in Gran Canaria's north. Agaete, Galdar and Arucas are the centres of agricultural production. Mainly citrus fruits and bananas are farmed here for domestic use as well as export. Terraced farming is, however, relatively limited on the island. It is covered extensively with oasis-like settlements, for instance those between Ingenio and Agüimes, surrounded by a ring of irrigated or non-irrigated fields. In winter, tomatoes and corn are planted. Windmills pump water from the wells; pozos rotate on high steel towers bringing water to those areas where too little can be found on the surface.

In contrast, there are certain regions like that around Firgas that have such a large amount of drinking water that it is bottled and exported to the neighbouring islands.

With the dimensions of a huge cañon, the Barranco de Tejeda between the steep canyon walls

Gran Canaria is foremost an agricultural island; even the capital of Las Palmas can be considered agricultural. However, all the blessings and horrors common for a harbour city of this size have set root here. There are numerous hotels and apartments as well as diverse entertainment from the long sandy beach Playa de la Canteras to discotheques and night clubs in which minors are not admitted. Las Palmas is considered one of the pivotal point for international drug trafficking. The newspaper articles dedicated to heroin or cocaine seizures continually shrink in size although the drug trafficker is sent to prison for several years not to mention a fine in the millions.

Returning to agriculture: between Galdar and Puerto San Nicolas, tomatoes are grown in the middle of this banana region. There are no fruit trees in this area, but there are fields where the opuntia species of cactus are grown — remnants from the cochineal farming. The red pigment carmesine used in making cosmetics is obtained from the larvae of these lice which live off of the cactus, a pigment which is still used occasionally today. Between the cactus fields are large round cisterns or "tanques" containing the most precious commodity — water. The cisterns are sometimes surrounded by earthen canals used in irrigation and running all across the land.

The southern portion of the island is especially considered to have a sunshine guarantee. However, it is also more barren in comparison to the central and northern regions with their lush vegetation. The visitor will find himself in a desert landscape similar to the Sahara near Maspalomas, Playa del Ingles, San Andres and Puerto Rico. There are, however, other coastal sections where golden sandy beaches can also be found.

Guanches

It is almost impossible to avoid contact with the Guanche culture in some way or other on the Canary Islands. This group of people have not only left behind relics like mummified corpses, caves and pieces of pottery but also a marked influence on the language. Those Canarians who are tall, with light coloured hair and blue eyes might likely be able to trace their ancestry back to the original inhabitants of the Canary Islands.

The fortunate islands, "insulae fortunatae" were such a paradise that they were not only of interest to the Romans or Greeks. In 1400 B.C., it is said that the Egyptian king Sesostris visited the Guanches on this group of islands. The fact that there were actually islands in the Atlantic was something that the world would once more forget — this, with the exception of the Guanches. And they, on the other hand, were not aware of the world beyond the limits of their islands. They had no boats. It was only in the 15th century that this limited perception of the world was questioned. The French arrived at this time to be followed somewhat later by the Spaniards. Their visit was a loud, clear and deadly signal: they arrived heavily armed. These were after all the conquerors (→*History*). What the conquerors were to find on the island was a Stone Age culture in which pottery techniques were quite advanced although basic, and the weapons simple. With the arrival of the Spaniards on the Canary Islands, the original inhabitants would soon become known as the Guanches. This term is only really applicable to the people of Tenerife, the island which was originally called "Guancherfe." "Quan" was A Guanche for "a son " and this, not any son but a son of this island.

The Spaniards killed many Guanches; others they married. The dragon which was presumed to guard the islands of bliss, the islands of Hesperides, is long since forgotten — unless it is sleeping somewhere under the surface of this volcanic island. Only a few words and phrases remain as remnants of the Guanche language.

The king had the say on the islands. If a conflict were to develop, then it would probably have to do with the rights to the land which were allocated to the farmers and shepherds. The aristocracy owned sheep, goats, pigs and rabbits. Farmers' wives worked the fields with tools made of obsidian, a volcanic, glass-like mineral.

If the fields were overcultivated, this did not concern the farmers — they did not even irrigate them. It was far simpler to move on and find a new, fertile tract of land. Those who did not want to farm or tend livestock, could earn their livelihood through fishing. The fish were driven into the bays and then bludgeoned with sticks.

The Guanches were predominantly vegetarians, eating for the most part vegetables and Gofio. The grain for Gofio was roasted, ground and then extended with water, goat's milk or lard and then spun in a goat leather bag until the proper doughy consistency was achieved. This could be eaten raw or dissolved in warm water. Today, Gofio is still a nutritious staple in the Canarian diet, made from freshly roasted grain.

Guantanamo →*Tauro*
Guest Houses →*Accommodation*

Guia

The complete name of Guia, 5 kilometres (3 miles) east of Galdar, is Santa Maria de Guia de Gran Canaria. The shorter version is far less complicated and just as widely understood. From here, it is only a few miles to Cenobio de Valeron, the fascinating Guanche caves.

On the way to the caves, one must drive along the road number 810 further to Las Palmas. A considerable distance before leaving town, there is a sign on the left-hand side of the street for the well known Queso Flor de Guia. Here a mild and a more intensive tasting cheese, made of goat's and cow's milk is sold — marketed under this name. Both types of cheese are treated with various plant extracts.

The older gentleman behind the counter is quite generous with samples of the products as well as of wines and cornbread. Of course the main intent is still to sell these products and the prices are quite fair. Those who do not wish to purchase these delicacies can also buy goats wool here for £7 ($12). This is not only intended as a souvenir, but is actually used in agriculture. Other articles sold here are pottery and other farming tools typical to this region.

Accommodation: Located in Guia is one of the two youth hostels (alberge juvenil) on Gran Canaria. It is call "Residencia San Fernando" and the international youth hosted identification card is obligatory. To get to the youth hostel, one must go to the church in town and continue west along the main street. Price: £2.35 ($4.15) per person per night. Full board costs £6 ($10). The cafeteria is not open to the public. The youth hostel has 40 beds, most of which are in four-bed rooms. The courtyard is a lovely place to relax in the sunshine. The youth hostel is simply furnished.

Pharmacy: Calle Perez Galdos

Restaurants: There are a number of restaurants on the through street, including the inexpensive "Tiscamanta."

Service Station: On the through street to Las Palmas de Gran Canaria.

Güigüi

Güigüi, or Güigüi Chico, is a beach southwest of San Nicolas de Tolentino and for many young travellers *the* beach on Gran Canaria. Güigüi is accessible from Tasartico only on foot. Tasartico is a settlement to the left of the old footpaths branching off of the main street. To get to the footpaths, one must bear left after Tasarte when heading toward Mogan. A second and much longer footpath leads from Puerto de San Nicolas along the 790 metre high (2,583 feet) Montaña del Cedro to the canyon Barranco de Güigüi Grande. To get to the beach, one must first wait for low tide, then the hike continues around a cliff formation which is normally surrounded by water.

Güigüi is a semicircular bay with sunshine from 11 o'clock in the morning. The freshwater waterfalls provide water for only for the fewest of visitors. Algae have tainted the flavour of the water quite noticeably. Other than this, Güigüi has remained a paradise offering both the advantages and disadvantages of a paradise. The fewest of those deciding to sleep under the palm branches will want forgo the comforts of civilisation — like food. And this is also the cause of the debris which has collected, like plastic bottles from the Firgas wells. There is also hardly any fire wood near Güigüi — once a well kept secret, word is now out. Debris is collected behind a small wall to at least preserve some appearance of paradise.

During low tide, one can walk to a farm house where a farmer's wife has adapted to the young visitors. She sells cheese, eggs and bread, sometimes even drinking water. Those planning to stay for a longer period of time on the bay of Güigüi must plan on going to the nearest villages with their backpacks every 14 days to stock up on supplies. Where the necessary supplies are available, one would expect to also find the necessary facilities. However, there are not yet toilets on this beach.

Health Insurance

It is recommended to take out a travel health insurance policy for the duration of the trip (→*Insurance*).

The Spanish physicians will charge directly for treatment. Upon returning home, one must present invoices for medical treatment and medication to the insurance company. For this reason, one should always ask for an invoice after visiting a clinic, hospital or doctor's office.

History

The geological age of Gran Canaria is estimated at 16 million years, making this island somewhat older than Tenerife (15 million years) and much younger than Fuerteventura (38 million years) and Lanzarote (19 million years).

Scriptures from Arabian geographers report of visits to the Canary Islands as early as 999 A.D. Ben-Farroukh was a captain from Lusitania, now Portugal, and heard of extraordinarily beautiful islands off the Libyan coast. This elicited his interest and, a short time later together with 130 of his men, he arrived on Gran Canaria near where the airport of Gando is located today.

Ben-Farroukh explored the island thoroughly, hiked through the dense forests and steep valleys. He finally arrived in Galdar to be received by the Guanarteme Guanariga, the king and his advisors and ministers. They feasted together and the discussed the possibility of making Gran Canaria a haven for Ben-Farroukh's boats, should they be threatened by pirates. The captain sang the praises of his host upon his return to Lisbon. The people of the Canary Islands were most civilised with a highly developed social order, exemplary agricultural methods and exceptional craftsmen. Gran Canaria, along with the other islands, was soon forgotten despite this praise. It was only in 1360 that two galleys with crews from Mallorca and Aragon entered the harbour of Gando. The seamen were incautious and went too far into the interior of the island. Because their intentions were unclear, they were taken prisoner by the natives. Five Franciscan monks were among them. The monks won the trust of the Guanches by planting fig trees and building comfortable houses. However, they misjudged the favour of their hosts. In their religious fervour to convert the natives to Christianity, they behaved badly, injuring the honour of the Guanches. The Guanches felt forced to condemn the monks to death by throwing them from the cliffs — an execution reserved for adulterers and traitors.

On October 6, 1405, ships set off anew for Gran Canaria. No less than Juan de Bethancourt, Baron of Saint Martin de Gaillard in the county of Eu de Normandie, whose goal was to conquer the island. Prior to this, he had great success in conquering Lanzarote and Fuerteventura. He was gradually working his way westward.

On Gran Canaria, so he had heard, he would have to contend with 10,000 dedicated warriors. He, on the other hand, had only three galleys, albeit with well-armed soldiers. A storm drove their ship ashore on the African coast — all the way to Cape Bojador. Instead of battling with the Guanches, he abducted several natives and three thousand camels which he planned to bring to Fuerteventura and Lanzarote. One of the galleys, the one with Juan de Bethancourt aboard, was driven by a storm to Gran Canaria. The second landed on La Palma, the third met up with the first after a detour to Fuerteventura. Despite the fact that Bethancourt had expressly prohibited this, the knight Quillome de Auberbose set off for the islands interior with 45 men. They were subsequently attacked by the Guanches. The surviving Spaniards regrouped on the coast and set off with their leader Bethancourt for El Hierro, the southwestern island of the archipelagos.

The next attempt took place in 1461. Diego García de Herrera, the successor and son-in-law Fernan Peraza, who died in 1452, formed a troop under the orders of Diego de Silvas for an expedition to Gran Canaria. The soldiers pushed on all the way to Galdar and would have been defeated by the more powerful Guanches, had the Guanarteme not halted his enraged warriors. Upon this, Herrera took up contact with the Guanarteme of Telde and was granted permission to build a fortress in this region.

However, the Canarians soon realised that the fort was directed against them. They dressed in the uniforms they had taken from fallen Spaniards, stole into the fort and destroyed it, killing a number of their opponents. Three of the islands in the Canarian archipelagos had still not submitted to the Castillian crown as late as 1472: La Palma, Tenerife and Gran Canaria.

The opposition on Gran Canaria was feared the most because the inhabitants on this island had come out victorious from all of the previous Spanish attacks. Because problems are best solved by eliminating them, this island was attacked first.

In 1478, the preparations were so advanced that Juan Rejon could set foot in Las Palmas on June 24. His two most powerful opponents were the Guanartemes of Telde and Galdar. The first was named Doramas; the latter, Tenesor Semidan. To combat Rejon, they joined forces, forming a well equipped army of warriors numbering over 2,000. Among them were Adargoma and Maninidra, whose names would go down in history.

Juan Rejon first tried the weak argument, that he was sent by the Catholic queen to convert the Canarians to the Christian faith. If they were to submit, then they would be under the protection of the Castillian crown — and, he added, the Canarians would be persecuted and enslaved for the rest of their lives if they were to refuse.

All of this did not set well with the Guanches. They had no slaves in their social structure. A new belief? The old belief had always functioned quite well. The Guanartemes answered diplomatically: "you will get your answer. Later." On the next day, directly after sunrise, Doramas gave the order to attack. The battle, called "Guiniguada," took place in the Guiniguada Canyon near Las Palmas. This battle cost a number of Canarians their lives. One historian speaks of 30, another of 300 casualties. Among the seriously wounded was Adargoma, who was then taken prisoner by the Spaniards.

Months went by. The Spaniards fortified their camp, Juan Rejon and the deacon Juan Bermudez, who had come over from Lanzarote fell into conflict. The spiritual adviser accused Rejon of delaying the conquest of Gran Canaria and not giving his men enough rations. While the attacked sought support against the church official on Lanzarote in vain, Bermudez demanded a new governor of the Catholic kings. Juan Rejon was sent back to Spain as a prisoner; Pedro de Algaba became the new governor of the island.

Rejon did not quietly watch as his power was being continually reduced. He reestablished himself in Spain and travelled back to Gran Canaria. A new bishop named Frias, supplies, ammunition and new soldiers were aboard his ships. However, Frias' attempts to reconcile Rejon, de Algaba and Bermudez failed: Rejon returned to Cadiz and waited for a more opportune moment.

On August 24, 1479, it was too peaceful on the island for Algaba. The Guanches still would not submit to his royally appointed authority. He landed on a section of the coast, which he thought would make a good base for his attack on Tirajana and then marched into the mountains to the present-day San Bartolome de Tirajana. The Guanches hid and set a military trap, surprising their opponents. They slew 26 men and injured over 100. Counting the few Spanish prisoners, the total came to a loss of 80 men.

This was the moment for which Rejon had been waiting. The fact that Algaba could be so capricious as to fall into such a trap encouraged him. Driven by revenge, he returned to Gran Canaria and brutally occupied the fort and the cathedral of Las Palmas. In a quick trial, he had de Algaba beheaded the next morning and he banished Deacon Bermudez from the country. Easy come, easy go: Queen Isabella was so touched by the widow de Algaba's tears and so convinced that Rejon's behaviour was inappropriate that she replaced him with Pedro de Vera. She had had enough of the constant quibbling of her subjects — and that, in 1480.

De Vera was an Andalusian Lieutenant General of Jerez de la Frontera and Castille of Jimena. He would know how to avoid political power struggles. He came with three ships, 150 riflemen, and 20 horses on August 18, 1480. De Vera was also a strategic expert and decided to first push into the north, conquering Galdar, the residence of Doramas.

The Guanarteme had no chance against the overwhelming forces; before being stabbed by Pedro de Vera, he was able to physically overpower one Spaniard. Diego de Hoza, who fought at the side of his leader, seriously wounded Doramas in the back. Doramas collected his last strength and broke the cowardly attacker's leg. He was then mortally wounded by de Vera in the chest, calling Diego de Hoza a traitor.

Pedro de Vera saw the surviving Guanches retreating to the mountains. In September of 1481, he ordered his prisoners to build a fortress in Agaete, which he — together with 30 men under the leadership of Alonso Fernandez de Lugo — used to gather some experience he would later need in conquering Tenerife. Once again, the Spaniards attacked the Guanches, lost 25 men and decided it was better to retreat to Las Palmas with their wounded. There, they would find no peace — especially not from Bentagay.

One day, the Guanche came to the camp under the pretence of wanting to be baptised. He inspected the quarters and stalls of the Spaniards and disappeared only to return at night. He wanted to cause as much damage as possible — and quite a lot was possible.

Pedro de Vera had now won the support of another conquistador, the relentless Count of Valdeflores. Fernan Peraza had become famous through his attempts to conquer the island of La Gomera. Together, they marched to Galdar. For Tenesor Semidan and 15 of his most trusted men, the attack came as a complete surprise. The were found in a cave, having been taken prisoner, and

Semidan even consented to be baptised. His name would now become Fernando Guanarteme, or also Fernando de Galdar. The last and highly respected Guanche king had been forced to submit to Spanish rule.

However, there was still an enclave called Ansite between Tirajana and Galdar, which served as a haven for women and children, who had gone into hiding, led by Bentejuis. The Guanarteme talked his "subjects" into surrendering. Some laid down their weapons, but many women threw themselves from the cliffs, fearing Spanish slavery. Bentejuis and the Faycan, a high priest, drown themselves together in the sea — this, according to one version. Another version reports that they threw themselves into a canyon in an embrace. The result was the same: on April 29, 1483, the conquest of Gran Canaria had come to a conclusive end.

Now it was up to the Spaniards to divvy up the spoils. Some of the soldiers who had come to the island with Pedro de Vera, later with Alonso Fernandez de Lugo or even with Fernan Peraza were sent back to Spain or hired for the conquest of further islands. New settlers came and were given generous shares in the exploitation of the island's riches. The Land Allocation Act, the Datas,

Folk dances are an integral part of every festival

documents that 30 settlers were given larger estates and water rights. The Guanches were not to be left empty handed either: they were not forgotten, being taken into account in the allocation of their island.

Holiday Apartments →*Accommodation*

Holidays and Celebrations

General Holidays: In addition to Maundy Thursday, Good Friday, Christmas Eve, Easter, Christ's Ascension, Pentecost and Corpus Christi:

January 1: New Year's Day
January 6: Epiphany, celebrated with presents for the children; parades and processions on all of the islands
March 14: St. Joseph's Day
April 1: Day of Victory in the Civil War
May 1: Labour Day
May 30: Dia de Canarias
June 29: Peter and Paul
July 18: Anniversary of the National Uprising
July 25: St. Jacob's Day (patron saint of Spain)
August 15: Mary's Ascension
October 12: Anniversary of the discovery of America ("Dia da Raza")
November 1: All Saint's Day
December 8: Immaculate Conception
December 25: Christmas Day

Gran Canaria / Holidays and Celebrations
January 29: In Agüimes a parade with festive costumes and flowers in honour of the "winter queen."
February: Almond blossom festival in Tejeda.
April 20: Sporting events and celebrations in Las Palmas commemorating the incorporation of Gran Canaria in the Castille Empire.
May/June: Corpus Christi festival with carpets of flowers at the Santa Ana Cathedral as well as parades in Las Palmas and Arucas.
July 16: Fiestas del Carmen at the harbour Puerto de la Luz in Las Palmas, Galdar, and San Bartolome de Tirajana.
August 5: Procession of the branches ("Bajada de la Rama") in honour of "Nuestra Señora de las Nieves." Fireworks, games, sporting events.
August 15: Festival in honour of the patron saint Santa Maria de Guia in Guia.
September 6 to 8: "Mud Festival" in San Nicolas de Tolentino.

October 6: Festival in the harbour of Las Palmas de Gran Canaria commemorating the Canarians' victory over Sir Francis Drake in 1595.
Last Sunday in October: Festival of St. Olaf, king of Norway, in Las Roses near Agüimes.
November 30: Fiesta del Rancho del Animas in Teror.
November 30: Aquatic procession in honour of the "Virgin of Candelaria" in Las Palmas. The virgin of light is the patron saint of Puerto de la Luz.

Hospitals →*Medical Care*

Ingenio

As is the case with the neighbouring city of Agüimes, the village of Ingenio in the central eastern portion of Gran Canaria has a typically Arabian flair. Earlier, this was the centre of sugar cane production on Gran Canaria. Today, Canarian embroidery is produced in a school next to the Museo de Piedras y Artesania, which is then sold at a much higher price in Las Palmas. Therefore, it is best to purchase these articles here. The museum and the embroidery school are open from 8 am to 6 pm; admission is free of charge. The embroidery school is not easily found. One exits the city on the main street toward Las Palmas. After a little over half a mile, one will see a building to the right with two white turrets and Spanish flags. This is the building. In back, there is also a small palm garden. Inside the building there is also a bar.
Running south from Ingenio is the Barranco de Agüimes in which Guanche tombs were found. Some of the mummies can be seen in the Museo Canario in Las Palmas.
When Ingenio and Agüimes are compared, the beautiful city of Ingenio usually comes out on top, due to its clean and orderly inner city.
Across from the town hall is the Church de la Candelaria with a dome similar to that of a mosque. This church is located on the Plaza bordered by palm trees, laurel trees and geraniums. The way to the town hall is marked by the "Ayuntamiento" sign from the intersection of Calle de Leon y Castillo/Calle General Primo de Rivera. On the spacious plaza in front of the town hall, there is a fountain embellished with four frogs.
Currency Exchange: Caja Insular, Plaza de la Candelaria, next to the town hall. Banco Español, Calle de Leon y Castillo, Banco Hispáno Americano on the through street.
Entertainment: Discotheque "Maipe," Calle 1. de Abril.
Pharmacy: Calle de Leon y Castillo.

Insurance

Supplemental health insurance for the duration of one's stay on Gran Canaria is a good idea. Some insurance companies also offer a travel package with insurance coverage for everything from liability, accidents, theft and lost luggage.

International Press

Newspapers in the English language are available on the islands of Lanzarote, Fuerteventura, Gran Canaria, Tenerife and La Palma in the larger cities and tourist centres — this, however, with a delay of at least one day. Also among the selection are national and international magazines. On El Hierro and La Gomera, finding newspapers and magazines in English can be somewhat more difficult.

News papers and magazines can be purchased at the newsstands and in the "Librerías."

On the large islands, there are magazines and newspapers produced especially for tourists, for instance "Canarias Tourist" or "Lanzarote." In these papers, tips and trends on the islands are covered as well as giving businesses the opportunity to advertise. These newspapers and magazines cost between 35p (60cents) and £3.50 ($4.25).

Gran Canaria / International Press

Other than the newspapers in English, which are flown in from the British Islands, there are also other important publications printed on the island. "Canarias Tourist" is a comprehensive, informative paper, appearing bimonthly. Each article is printed in English, German, Dutch and Swedish — in the languages that most of the holiday visitors on Gran Canaria speak. "Canarias Tourist" costs around £1 ($1.75). One can also subscribe to "Canarias Tourist" for £25 ($45) for twelve months by contacting: "Canarias Tourist," Edificio Mercurio, Torre 1, Planta 7F, Playa de Ingles, Gran Canaria.

Isleta →*Las Palmas*
Jardin Botanico →*Botanical Garden*

La Atalaya

Between Santa Brigida and Telde, the narrow road GC 380 leads through the canyon Barranco de la Cruz to La Atalaya. In this village, situated at a high elevation, various potters produce ceramic goods using the same methods that were used by the Guanches many years ago. The Guanches had no potter's wheel, that constructed the pots from a clump of reddish clay using a wooden stick. The sides were then smoothed and the pots fired. The location of La Atalaya makes it suited for defence. From this town, the surrounding plains were watched and enemies — whether Guanches, Spaniards or merely thieves — could be seen at quite a distance.

The Bandama Golf Course can also be found in La Atalaya.

La Caleta

One of the longest sections of beaches — although less developed for tourists — can be found near La Caleta, south of Agüimes. The Castillo de Romeral in La Caleta was one of the first fortresses on Gran Canaria. However, those who expect the fortress complex to be obvious will be disappointed. Today, Castillo is a district of the city whose original character can only be recognised by its layout.

Serpentine: the mountain pass near La Atalaya

Language

Although the official language on Gran Canaria is Spanish, the two other widely spoken languages are English and German. Many announcements are made in English and numerous waiters will be able to communicate in English. Being able to speak even a little Spanish will still be advantageous, not only as a courtesy. It is also quite fun to have a command of at least a little of this fiery, temperamentally spoken language — even if it goes slowly and stuttered. The Canarians are thankful even if the visitor merely makes an effort to speak their language. In more remote towns, it is even a necessity to speak some Spanish. Resourceful gestures or pantomiming are always helpful.

A small Spanish dictionary should definitely be brought along — if all else fails, one can always point to the appropriate word. The pronunciation of the Spanish language is relatively easy:

Phrases

Mister	Señor
Mrs.	Señora
Ladies and Gentlemen	Señoras y señores
Do you speak English/Spanish?	Habla Usted ingles/español?
Yes, I speak... No, I do not speak...	Si, hablo... No, no hablo...
Yes, a little.	Si, un poco.
Good Morning! God Day! (until noon)	Buenos días.
Good Day! Good Evening (until dusk)	Buenos tardes.
Good Night!	Buenos noches.
See you soon!	Hasta pronto! Hasta luego!
See you this evening!	Hasta la noche!
Good bye!	Adios!
Yesterday, today, tomorrow	ayer, hoy, mañana
How are you?	Como esta? or Que tal?
I am fine/not so good	Me va bien/mal.
I am not doing too well.	No me siento bien.
My name is ...	Mi nombre es ...
I wear glasses	Tengo un deseo
why?	Por que?
what is wrong? what has happened?	Que pasa?
Where is...?	Donde queda

the nearest post office?	la proxima oficina de correos?
the police station?	el puesto de policía
the hospital?	el hospital?
the pharmacy?	la farmacia
Yes, no	si, no
please	por favor
Yes, that's possible	es posible
Thank you.	Gracias.
Excuse me!	Perdone!
No problem. Don't mention it.	No importa. De nada.
What time is it?	Que hora es?
I am hungry/thirsty.	Tengo hambre/sed.
I would like to have something to eat.	Quisiera / Me gustaria comer algo
How much does this cost?	Cuanto cuesta esto?
What would you like?	Que desea Usted?
Do you have...?	Tiene Usted?
half a pound	media libre
kilogramme	kilo
a bottle of red/white wine	una botella de vino blanco/tinto

Numbers

0 = cero, 1 = uno/una, 2 = dos, 3 = tres, 4 = cuatro, 5 = cinco, 6 = seis, 7 = siete, 8 = ocho, 9 = nueve, 10 = diez, 11 = once, 12 = doce, 13 = trece, 14 = catorce, 15 = quince, 16 = dieciseis, 17 = diecisiete..., 20 = veinte, 21 = veintiuno/veintiuna, 22 = veintidos, 30 = treinta, 40 = cuarenta, 50 = cincuenta, 60 = sesenta, 70 = setenta, 80 = ochenta, 90 = noventa, 100 = ciento, 101 = ciento uno/ciento una, 200 = doscientos/-as, 1000 = mil.

Lanzarote

The road GC 110 leads to Lanzarote shortly beyond Valleseco on the way to Cruz de Tejeda. This is a small farming village, in which one can find quite reasonably priced products. This is especially true in the small shops across from the garage on the sharp curve in the road. The shop has no distinctive sign; the peanuts and figs are highly recommended.

The lady who owns the shop is extremely helpful and even has the neighbours help if customers arrive at a less convenient time of day during the siesta. The bakery is not far from here, but difficult to find. It is closed during the midday siesta. In the grocery shops, foreign visitors are assisted with patience and courtesy. The anonymity of a department store is diametrically opposed to this personable atmosphere.

La Plata

La Plata is one of the many small settlements between Tejeda and San Bartolome. Another of these is Ayacata. Ayacata can be reached from Tejeda via the road 811 heading south. The town consists of a few restaurants and souvenir shops. When continuing on the trip one will drive through La Plata which is a collection of farmhouses scattered beneath the cliffs. The road leading left from the intersection in town goes to Agualatente and Risco Blanco, a white cliff which seems to be embedded in the mountainside. The Risco Blanco is a good reason for a short trip to La Plata. What will surprise many visitors is the number of dogs, which seem to chase anything that is motorised.

Las Casas de Veneguera *→Veneguera*

Las Lagunetas

Located halfway between San Mateo and Cruz de Tejeda, to the north of road GC 814, is Las Lagunetas. This picturesque village in the canyon Barranco de Mina consists of several farms located among the foothills. The residents make their livelihood by farming the fertile fields in the lush, green valley. **Restaurants:** In worldly contrast to the church is the bar "Hermanos Moreno" located next door to it. Las Lagunetas is quite a distance from the nearest towns and villages. The bar, run by the Moreno brothers, serves an important role as a meeting place, where young men can meet young women under the watchful supervision of the older men and women of the village. Not all the young people of the village have access to a car, making it possible to escape this surveillance.

Las Palmas

Located in the extreme northeast of Gran Canaria is one of the largest harbours of Europe: Puerto de la Luz. This is a very important harbour for the shipping traffic between America, Europe and Africa. It holds all of the horrors and enticements of the big city: significant social contrasts from wealth to poverty, traffic jams, nonstop entertainment on the harbour promenade, and a crime rate which certainly makes one worry about one's wallet. Cars are broken into regularly, even during the daytime; leaving even a few bags in a locked car within view can attract the attention of thieves.

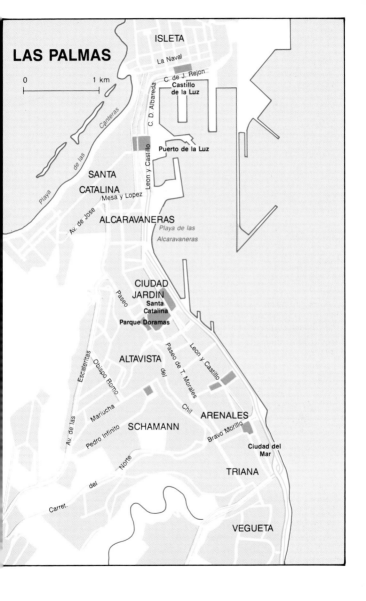

The island's capital has international flair with numerous museums, the Santa Ana Cathedral and two, usually heavily crowded beaches. Over 360,000 residents live in this city, the capital of the Gran Canaria province, which includes the islands of Gran Canaria, Fuerteventura and Lanzarote. This is over half of the total population of Gran Canaria.

Las Palmas / **Sights**

The peninsula Isleta, with its volcanic basalt and lava, is connected with the main portion of Gran Canaria by a narrow isthmus to the north of the city. In the 19th century, the harbour *Puerto de la Luz* was built, one of the most important harbours in Spain, Europe and the world. On the one hand, Puerto de la Luz is located near the fishing regions between the Sahara and the islands. On the other hand, it is a free harbour and freight forwarding harbour for goods being transported to and from Europe. There are regular ship connections to mainland Spain, Hamburg, Bremen, Bremerhaven and Genoa as well as to the other Canary Islands.

The Isleta begins north of the two mile long *Las Canteras* and to the south of the beach *Alcavaneras* — two of the most important tourist attractions in Las Palmas. Hotels, discotheques, shops and bazaars line the harbour promenade. Those who would rather not swim can observe the colourful bustle from one of the many beach cafés.

The canyon *Barranco Guiniguada* divides Las Palmas into a younger, modern northern and an older, stately southern district, the *Vegueta*.

The first to land here were the Spaniards under the leadership of Genera Juan de Rejon, who was to push on into the islands interior in 1478 and later conquer Gran Canaria. Juan de Rejon began the construction of Las Palmas in 1478 in founding Villa Real de Las Palmas in a palm grove on the right banks of the Barranco.

Four large bronze statues of dogs have been standing guard on the *Plaza Santa Ana* in front of the Santa Ana Cathedral. These dogs have little in common with the authentic Canarian dogs, which could have given the group of islands its name. The authentic Canarian dogs are sooner small and puny and are only represented as thoroughbreds in the United States.

The construction of the Santa Ana Cathedral began in 1497 and lasted well into the 18th century with numerous interruptions and under the direction of a number of different architects. In 1570, the builders interrupted work. A part of the Cathedral was completed at that time in Gothic architecture and opened for religious services. The facade facing the Santa Ana Plaza is in neo-classicist style with two bell towers on each side and a balcony in the middle. The building is comprised of three arched naves supported by slender columns. In addition to the flag of the conquest, inside are also valuable paintings and sculptures, some dating back to the 15th century. Religious services and the times that the cathedral's treasury are open are: Monday to Friday 6 to 10:30 am, Saturdays 7 to 10:30 am and 7 to 9 pm, on Sundays and holidays 7 to 1:30 pm and 6:30 to 8 pm.

On the corner of Calle Dr. Chil and Calle Dr. Verneau is the *Museo Canario,* which visitors will especially find interesting because of its anthropological and archaeological exhibitions. It is the largest museum on all of the Canary Islands. In this museum, there are taxidermically prepared giant lizards "Lacerta simonyi," which could grow up to 24 inches (60cm). From the beginning of this century, they have been presumed to be extinct on all of the Canary Islands. They originate from the Tertiary Period, survived the volcanic formation of the islands; however, not the influence of mankind. The museum is open Mondays to Fridays from 10 am to 1 pm and from 3 to 6 pm, Saturdays from 10 am to noon. It is closed on holidays. Admission: £1.50 ($2.65).

The *Teatro Perez Galdos* on the Calle Bravo Murillo was named after the famous Canarian author, who was born in 1843 and lived in Las Palmas up to 1920. He wrote the 46-volume work "Episodios Nacionales" and left behind almost 400 illustrations relating to this work. The theatre can accommodate an audience of 1,400. During the summer months, operas are often performed.

The house where Perez Galdos was born is the *house number 30* on Cano Street, not far from the theatre. Today, it is a museum in honour of this author. Open 9 am to noon, closed Sundays and holidays.

In the *Santa Antonio Abad,* Columbus is said to have prayed the last time before departing on his discoveries.

The main shopping street is also located in the neighbouring district of San Telmo, the *Calle Mayor de Triana.* Earlier, this was the centre for simple craftsmen and merchants, but then more land was reclaimed from the ocean, and the business centre expanded significantly. International firms with exclusive fashions, specialty shops and department stores have settled in this district, selling mostly luxury articles. The Calle Mayor de Triana runs parallel to the Avenida Maritima del Sur in the proximity Muelle de Las Palmas.

The northern portion of Las Palmas between Vegueta and Isleta: On the fishing harbour Muelle Santa Catalina is also the *Parque Santa Catalina,* a refreshing, lively area where a bit of the Canarian tranquillity has remained intact. Here, there are numerous cafés, bars, bazaars, newsstands, peddlers and the bus stop for three of the main bus lines (corner of Calle Leon y Castillo). The Casa del Tourismo, the information centre for visitors, is also located here next to a small service station.

Located at the beginning of the Isleta, after crossing the isthmus on the Leon y Castillo street, is the fortress *Castillo de la Luz,* the fortress of light. It is a crude block, without the elegance of central European fortresses. The Castillo served the Spaniards as a point of departure during the conquest of the island in the 15th century. It then served to protect the city from pirate attacks from Holland and England for over 200 years. Today, those curious enough to want to visit the Castillo will probably be driven away by the smell of the fish processing industry.

The "garden city" of *Ciudad Jardin* and *Parque Doramas* can be found by heading toward the island's interior on the main street Leon y Castillo. These were named after the last of the island's Guanche leaders. This is also the location of the luxury hotel "Santa Catalina," with its complex architecture in Canarian style. It was built in 1953.

A casino has been adjacent to the Santa Catalina since December 15, 1987. With a total of 8,600 square feet, 60 croupiers imported from England run the gambling tables. The casino was furnished at a cost of almost £2 million ($3.5 million). At the point in time when the casino was opened, it was not clear

The Santa Ana Cathedral in Las Palmas: artists and architects of various eras have left their mark on this building

whether the Spanish government would grant the owners a gambling licence. The land on which the casino was built is governmental property and a park was planned for this plot of land. In the *Pueblo Canario* in Parque Doramas, Canarian dances and songs are performed every Sunday from 11:45 am to 1:15 pm and Thursdays from 5:30 to 7:30 pm.

The permanent exhibition in the *Museo Nestor* in the Pueblo Canario displays paintings by Nestor de la Torre (1887 to 1938), who lived in this house and also designed the Pueblo Canario itself. His plans were then realised by the architect Miguel Marti. The Museo Nestor is open Monday to Friday from 10 am to noon and from 4 to 7 pm, Saturdays from 10 am to noon and Sundays from 10:30 am to 1:30 pm. Closed Wednesdays. Admission: 13p (25 cents).

Las Palmas / **Practical Information**
Accommodation

Hotel "Cristina"*****, Gomera 6, Tel: 26 76 00. 316 rooms; doubles from £74 ($130).

Hotel "Reina Isabel"*****, Alfredo L. Jones 40, Tel: 26 01 00. 234 rooms; doubles from £67 ($118).

Hotel "Santa Catalina"*****, Parque Dormas, next to the Pueblo Canario and with a casino, Tel: 24 30 40. 215 rooms; double rooms from about £97 ($171), the best hotel in the city.

Hotel "Los Bardinos"****, Eduardo Benot 3, Tel: 26 61 00. 215 rooms; doubles from £47 ($83).

Hotel "Concorde"****, Tomas Miller 85, Tel: 26 27 50. 127 rooms; doubles from £40 ($71).

Hotel Residencia "Iberia Sol"****, Avenida Maritima del Norte, Tel: 36 11 33. 298 rooms; doubles £50 ($89).

Hotel Residencia "Tigaday"*****, Ripoche 4, Tel: 26 47 20, 160 rooms from £25 ($45).

Hotel Residencia "Atlanta"***, Alfredo L. Jones 37, Tel: 26 50 62. 58 rooms from £17 ($30).

Hotel Residencia "Cantur"***, Sagasta 28, Tel: 26 23 04. 124 rooms; doubles from £24 ($41).

Hotel "Fataga"***, Nestor de las Torres 21, Tel: 24 04 08. 92 rooms from £37 ($65).

Hotel "Faycan"***, Nicolas Esevanez 61, Tel: 27 06 50. 61 rooms; doubles from £20 ($36).

Hotel "Gran Canaria"***, Playa de las Canteras, Tel: 27 50 78. 90 rooms from £34 ($59).

Hotel Residencia "Lumi"***, Colombia 12, Tel: 26 58 24. 61 rooms from £17 to £24 ($30 to $41).

Hotel Residencia "Miraflor"**, Dr. Grau Bassas 21, Tel: 26 16 00. 78 rooms from £17 to £24 ($30 to $41).

Hotel Residencia "Olympia"***, Dr. Grau Bassas 1, Tel: 26 17 20. 41 rooms from £20 to £24 ($36 to $41).

Hotel Residencia "Parque"***, Muelle de la Palmas 2, Tel: 26 80 00. 119 rooms from £34 ($59).

Hotel Residencia "Tenesoya"***, Los Martinez de Escobar 61, Tel: 27 07 00. 43 rooms from £24 ($41).

Hotel Residencia "Alva"****, Alfredo Jones 29, Tel: 26 42 28. 45 rooms from £17 ($30).

Hotel Residencia "Braemar"**, Luis Morote 29, Tel: 27 33 02. 44 rooms, doubles from £20 ($36).

Hotel Residencia "Guanapay"**, Pelayo 12, Tel: 26 22 50. 30 rooms from £10 ($18).

Hostal "España"*, Domingo J. Navarro 34, Tel: 36 09 60. 20 rooms from £12 ($21).

Guest House "Pacifico," Calle Sargento Llagos, £3.45 ($6), showers in the hallway, very clean, large light rooms, friendly proprietor, located in the pedestrian zone about 100 metres (110 yards) from the beach.

Hostal "Regina," Calle Ripoche 9, Tel: 26 42 79, £9 ($16), light rooms with high ceilings, nice lounge with television, owned by a friendly couple, located in the pedestrian zone.

The two above mentioned guest houses are special tips located in the new district.

Tips in the old district include:

Hostal "Sandra," Calle Naval 9, Tel: 26 26 00, £11 ($21), quiet location, rooms equipped with bathrooms, large rooms, 30 metres (33 yards) from the beach.

Hostal "Leonor," Calle Naval 73, £6 ($10), rooms equipped with bathrooms, some with a balcony, large rooms.

There are far more apartment complexes in Las Palmas de Gran Canaria than hotels. The complete list of these is available from the Tourist Information Offices. Some examples of the apartments available in Las Palmas in various categories are:

Apartments "Aguas Verdes" (three keys), Canteras 47, Tel: 26 84 50.
104 apartments, from £17 ($30) to £67 ($118).

Apartments "Herrera" (three keys), Dr. Apolinario Macias 4, Tel: 25 38 10. 6 apartments from £13.50 ($24).

Apartments "Laskibar" (three keys), Secretario Artiles 94, Tel: 26 03 54. 33 apartments, between £24 ($41) and £27 ($47).

Apartments "Arucas" (three keys), Pedro del Castillo 4, Tel: 26 24 82. 25 apartments, approximately £13.50 ($24).

Apartments "Brisamar-Canteras" (two keys), Playa de las Canteras 49, Tel: 26 94 00. 85 apartments, between £13.50 ($24) and £30 ($53).

Apartments "Catalina Park" (two keys), Tomas Miller 67, Tel: 26 41 24. 76 apartments between £13.50 ($24) and £20 ($36).

Apartments "Castillo Playa" (one key), Pedro del Castillo 18, Tel: 27 11 12. 24 apartments, between £13.50 ($24) and £17 ($30).

Apartments "La Coleta" (one key), Avenida las Canteras 58, Tel: 26 35 28. 14 apartments, between £11 ($19) and £14 ($25).

Apartments "Las Norias" (one key), Princesa Guayarmina 8, Tel: 26 87 14. 8 apartments, from £30 ($17.75).

Automobile Clubs

Real Automóvil Club de Gran Canaria, Leon y Castillo, 47-4, Tel: 36 61 88.
Touring Club de España, Hnos. Garcia de la Torre 2, Tel: 23 01 88.

Car Rental

"Carop Rent a Car" in the hotels "Metropol" and "Santa Catalina," Vegas 22.

"Autos Europa," Simon Bolivar 1 (Casa del Marino), Tel: 27 24 35.

"Cicar," Nicolas Estevanez 18 (near the park "Santa Catalina"), Tel: 27 72 13 and the "Jet Foil" station on the harbour Puerto de la Luz. Reservations can also be made by calling Tel: 27 72 13.

"Hertz," Sagasta 27/29, Tel: 26 45 76, 26 39 33 and 27 27 20.

"Orlando," Viriato 26, Tel: 27 69 50, 26 73 76, E. Maritima (Muelle Santa Catalina), Tel: 22 33 22.

"Occa" (Organizacion Canaria Coches Alquiler), Franchy y Roca 24 and the "Jet Foil" station at the harbour, Tel: 27 44 59 and 27 54 40.

"AVIS," Juan M. Duran 13, Tel: 26 55 67.

Currency Exchange

Banco Atlantico, Calle Franchy y Roca.
Banco Central, Fernando Guanarteme 2, Tel: 26 03 70.

Entertainment/Excursions

Excursions are offered by all travel agencies on Gran Canaria or through the hotels. Full day sangria parties are also offered, priced from £13.50 ($24) and include a nice trip to Maspalomas or Puerto Rico. Departure time from Las Palmas is between 9 and 11 am. One organiser is "Viajes Avitur, S.A." with two branch offices in Las Palmas: Nicolas Estevanez 55, Tel: 26 82 50 and Sagasta 7, Tel: 26 99 50.

Those who consider the trip to the party a little too complicated can find other options on the Promenade of Las Canteras at the beginning of the street Alfredo L. Jones 45 in the restaurant "Colon Playa" or in the pub "Rocco" on the street Dr. Miguel Rosa 20 (when coming from Las Canteras, take the street Luis Morote and continue to the right). A discotheque on the street Luis Morote is the "Zorbas," a night club, some of whose employees are already standing at the Santa Catalina Park recruiting clientele. The "Roman Night" is a mixture of burlesque reviews and exclusive cuisine — a treat for the eye as well as the palate.

Art galleries and exhibitions:

"Cairasco," Plaza de Cairasco 1.

"Castillo de la Luz," Juan Rejon, s/n.

"Circulo Mercantil," Leon y Castillo 57.

"Vegueta," Leon y Joven 17.

"Yles," Domingo J. Navarro.

Medical Care

Emergency unit, Paseo Tomas Morales, Tel: 24 51 57.

Hospital Insular, Avenida Maritima del Sur, Tel: 31 30 33.

British Hospital, Paseo de la Cornisa, Tel: 25 42 43.

Residencia Sanitaria "Nuestra Señora del Pino," Angel Guimera 87, Tel: 23 11 99.

International Clinic, Nuñez de Arce 2, Tel: 24 56 43.

British and American Clinic, Fagasta 5, Tel: 26 45 35.

Restaurants

On the promenade along the beach of Las Canteras, there are numerous cafés and restaurants. Quaint and colourful are also appropriate descriptions for the park bistro "Santa Catalina." In the "Placeta," there is live music, usually Spanish songs. A selection of restaurants:

"Don Quijote," Secretario Artiles 74, Tel: 27 83 17. Wide selection of food. For years, the speciality of this restaurant has been fondue Bourguignonne and tongue in champagne.

"Casa Julio," La Naval 132, Tel: 27 10 39. Open from 10 am to midnight. The fish dishes can be especially recommended.

"La Cabaña Criolla," Los Martinez de Escobar 37, Tel: 27 02 16. Open from 1 to 4 pm and from 8 pm to midnight. Specialising in Argentine grill dishes.

"House of Ming," Paseo de las Canteras 30, Tel: 27 45 63. Chinese Restaurant; speciality: boiled fish and leek, from £5 ($9).

What's new in the world? — a laid-back scene along the promenade in Las Palmas ▶

"Playa Chica" Restaurant, on the beach promenade Las Canteras is not expensive and the portions are large. Spanish cuisine.

"Kim," Alfredo L Jones 19, Tel: 26 40 57. Open from 6pm to midnight. The Scottish salmon is highly recommended.

Important Addresses

Tourist Information Office

Provincial Delegation of Information, Triana 70, Tel: 21 87 65.

Touristic Information Bureau, Casa del Tourismo, Parque Santa Catalina, Tel: 26 46 23.

Provincial Ministry for Information, Casa del Tourismo, Parque Santa Catalina, Tel: 27 07 90 and 27 16 00.

Centro de Iniciativas y Tourismo Pueblo Canario, Parque Doramas, Tel: 24 39 93.

Tourist Information Patronage of the Province, Leon y Castillo 17, Tel: 36 24 22 and 36 22 22.

Tennis Club Gran Canaria: Parque Doramas, Tel: 27 15 20.

Police: Plaza de Ingeniero Leon y Castillo, Tel: 36 11 86 and Augustin Millares 16, Tel: 31 08 87.

Taxi: Tel: 27 77 12, 27 77 53 and 31 85 38.

Post and Telegraph Office: General Franco 62, Tel: 36 13 20.

Telegrams by Telephone: Tel: 36 20 00.

Telephone Office (booths): General Primo de Rivera 11 and Domingo J. Navarro 30.

Iberia/Trasmediterranea

Avenida Ramirez Bethancourt, Tel: 37 21 11 and Avenida Maritima del Norte, Tel: 37 27 03.

"Viajes Canyrama," Nicolas Estevanez 49, Tel: 27 65 53, 27 66 06 and 27 67 08.

Spantax: Leon y Castillo 248-3; Tel: 24 15 49.

Airport Aviaco: Tel: 25 46 49.

Literature

Only one Canarian was to gain literary fame: Benito Perez Galdos (1843-1920). The theatre in Las Palmas de Gran Canaria was named in his honour. His series of novels "Episodios Nacionales" encompasses 46 volumes.

The first descriptions of the islands originate from the Italian engineer Leonardo Torriani (1590) and from Padre Espinosa (1595). The author Don Jose Viera y Clavio published three volumes in 1770: "Historia Generale de las Islas Canarias." These historical works have in part been translated into other languages (English and German). Further information is available in the book stores on the Canary Islands.

Los Palmitos →*Maspalomas*

Lucha Canaria

The Canarian form of wrestling has become the most popular sport on the islands — a sport which unique to the Canaries. Lucha is more than a simple wrestling match, by which a lot of dust is churned up. It is a sport with set rules and tradition, whereby a fair fight is emphasised, using all of the strength that a team can muster.

Two opposing teams confront each other, usually in an arena with a sand floor. Each team consists of twelve men, dressed in shirts and trousers which are rolled up above the calf. Within two minutes, the Luchadores try to force their opponents to the ground fighting individually. The team which has touched the ground twice with a part of their body other than the feet has lost.

The wrestlers pant, stomp and shove their opponent back and forth. Those who can, will try to trick their opponents. Experienced fighters know that the opponents shove only to provoke being shoved and then quickly dodge the shove, hoping that the opponent will lunge into emptiness, falling to the ground. The wrestlers bow low to the ground, trying to catch the others by the trousers. This is an advantage: then it is quite easy to pull the opponents legs out from under him at an opportune moment. The origin of this type of wrestling is not known. There are historians, who place the origin in ancient Egypt — and there was contact between Egypt and the Canary Islands thousands of years ago. This type of competitive sport takes place regularly in Telde, Agüimes, Guia, Galdar and in the Stadium Lopez Socas in Las Palmas. Information is available at the hotel receptions and from the tour organisations.

Maps

Maps are available free of charge from most of the car rental agencies, usually included in a wallet along with the registration papers. Normally, this is only a rough sketch on which only the main roads are included. A map with suggested tour routes is published by the tourist association of Las Palmas and is also available free of charge. This map, along with additional information, is available at the Spanish Tourist Information Offices.

The "Tourist Map — Gran Canaria — Fuerteventura and Lanzarote" costs £ 1.50 ($2.65) and has a scale of 1:150,000. This map includes sufficient information on the island of Gran Canaria. The legend is also in several languages. On the back of the map, there are entries regarding the sights on these three islands.

Also with a scale of 1:150,000 is the "hymsa" map (1987, Madrid and Barcelona) for Gran Canaria which includes the islands of Fuerteventura and Lanzarote as well. This map cost around £1.35 ($2.35) on the islands. On the back of the city maps of the capitals of the three islands in this province: Las Palmas de Gran Canaria (more detailed), Arrecife and Puerto del Rosario (practically useless).

The "Hildebrandt" holiday map is available for £2.50 ($4.40) also with the islands of Lanzarote, Fuerteventura and Gran Canaria. Gran Canaria is depicted in a scale of 1:100,000. Also on this map are the cities of Las Palmas, Maspalomas, Playa del Ingles and San Agustin. The map includes distance tables and brief travel suggestions in English, German and French.

The excursion map "Mapa de Gran Canaria — plano del Sur" by Manuel Brito Auyanet costs about £4.50 ($2.65). It includes the most important places on Gran Canaria in a large scale as well as the southern tourist centres of San Agustin, Maspalomas, Playa del Ingles, Puerto Rico and Las Palmas with numerous suggestions for accommodation.

A piece of the Sahara on Gran Canaria and one of the highlights on this island: the dunes of Maspalomas

With a scale of 1:100,000, the map "Gran Canaria" published by INSOR is sold for about £1.70 ($3). This map is of very good quality and also includes the roads suited for day trips.

Maspalomas

At the time of the Phoenicians and Arabs, the Oasis of Maspalomas was still a pristine bird paradise with lush palm groves, bulrushes, cane and reeds growing in the swampy soil. Even twenty years ago, it was still an oasis.

The construction of the city destroyed this wealth of vegetation. In this landscape of sand dunes, there are still a few oases — with hotel complexes amid the palm trees. Maspalomas is a sunshine paradise and, despite the mass tourism, is still relatively quiet and relaxing. Those who find Maspalomas a little too peaceful will find more diversion in the neighbouring beach resort of Playa del Ingles.

The splendid colours of the subtropical Palmitos Park

Maspalomas / **Sights**

Playa del Maspalomas is the region including the Oasis Maspalomas, the lighthouse Faro de Maspalomas and the golf course. From the Oasis Maspalomas, one can get to the area of Lagos de Maspalomas by passing the horse and camel farm. At this point, at the latest, one will no longer have the impression of being in Spain, but rather in a huge amusement park. And indeed: there is an amusement park — *Holiday World*.

Admission is only 67p ($1.20) and free for children under 12. The amusement park only gets expensive after entering the park. There are only a few attractions which are included in the admission price; for others, an extra price is charged.

Holiday World extends over an area of 14,000 square metres (150,700 square feet) and is the largest amusement park on the Canary Islands. The largest ferris wheel in Spain is also located here, measuring 27 metres (88 feet) in diameter. In addition, there are pirate ships, go-carts, an octopus as well as a roller coaster.

Cameras can be rented for £3.50 ($6). The park is open daily from 6 pm to midnight, on Saturdays and Sundays till 1am (closed Mondays). Also considered an attraction of Maspalomas is the *Go-Kart Park* which is located near the Los Palmitos bird sanctuary and the tennis hotel in the canyon Barranco de la Data. In the Go-Kart Park, there is a snack bar and cafeteria, but first and foremost small, speedy sports cars. Prices depend on the number of rounds driven: 10 and under pay £2.50 ($4.40) for ten rounds; those 18 and older pay £5 ($9). The park assumes no liability for accidents or injuries. Before starting, the driver must pay a deposit of £5 ($9). If one drives more rounds than have been paid in advance, this is deducted from the deposit. Somewhat less expensive are the water-gliders, small motor boats which can be used in the adjacent pond for £1 ($1.75). Driving further up the canyon, on the left-hand side across from the restaurant "El Alamo," is a *riding school*. 23 Hispano-Arabian horses are available by the hour for accompanied expeditions on horseback. The price: £7 ($12) to £9 ($15). Address: Carretera a Los Palmitos Park, Maspalomas, Gran Canaria, Tel: 76 02 09.

The riding school belongs to the *Rancho Park* which was established directly next to it. This is a restaurant in western style with a lively bullfighting arena. Admission for children £2.50 ($4.40), for adults £7.50 ($13.50). Sundays at 6 pm. After driving up the Barranco de la Data for 1¼ miles, one will come to the ornithological and botanical park *Los Palmitos*. The only park similar to it on the Canary Islands is the Loro Parque de la Cruz on Tenerife. Los Palmitos is a 22-hectare large, subtropical park complex with well-kept bird houses, colourful flower beds, small ponds and 45 different species of palm trees. A cross-section of the entire flora of this archipelagos is presented here. Near each specimen, there is a plaque containing information about the plant, making a visit to this park quite educational. A plant guide can be purchased for 25p (45 cents). Among the 1,200 species of exotic birds are striking peacocks, pheasants, flamingos, parakeets and humming birds. The parrots give a performance of their tricks lasting 25 minutes at 11:30 am and 12:30, 1:30, 3, 4 and around 5 pm.

The Palmitos Park is open daily from 9 am to 5:30 pm. Admission for adults is around £3.50 ($6), children between 4 and 12 pay around £2.25 ($4). There is bus service from Playa del Ingles from 9:30 am to 4:30 pm departing every 20 minutes; from San Agustin, approximately five times daily; from Puerto Rico, three times daily; and from Las Palmas, it is best to first go to Playa de Ingles and transfer to the buses there. A taxi from Los Palmitos park to San Agustin costs around £6 ($10); to Maspalomas or Playa del Ingles, around £5 ($9). In addition, in Oasis Maspalomas, golfers can try their skills on a golf course with 36 holes. The golf course is 3,236 metres (3,528 yards) in length; par 72. Tel: 76 25 81.

Maspalomas / **Practical Information**

Accommodation

Maspalomas is usually a destination for those who have booked package tours. The hotels, however, are not always full, making it possible to book a room when travelling through the area.

Hotel "Maspalomas Oasis"****, Playa de Maspalomas, Tel: 76 10 70. 342 rooms, £100 ($177) to £217 ($383).

Hotel "Apolo"****, Avenida de E.E.U.U. 28, Tel: 76 00 58. 115 rooms, between £47 ($83) and £77 ($136).

Hotel "Caserio"****, Avenida de Italia 8, Tel: 76 10 50. 106 rooms, from £40 ($71).

Hotel "Ifa Dunamar"****, Calle Helsinki 8, Tel: 76 12 00. 184 rooms, up to £100 ($177).

Hotel "Ifa Hotel Faro de Maspalomas"****, Playa Maspalomas, Tel: 76 04 62. 188 rooms, between £90 ($159) and £134 ($236).

Hotel "Lucana"****, Plaza del Sol s/n., Tel: 76 27 00. 167 rooms, between £40 ($71) and £50 ($89).

Hotel "Las Margaritas"****, Avenida de Gran Canaria 38, Tel: 76 11 12. 323 rooms; doubles between £40 ($71) and £77 ($136).

Hotel "Maspalomas Palm Beach"****, Avenida del Oasis s/n., Tel: 76 29 20. 385 rooms, around £167 ($295).

Hotel "Parque Tropical"***, Avenida Italia 1, Tel: 76 07 12. 235 rooms, between £34 ($59) and £90 ($159).

Hotel Residencia "Inter Club Atlantic"**, Jazmines 2, Tel: 75 09 50. 105 rooms, between 40 ($71) and £90 ($159).

Golf Club Maspalomas: Oasis de Maspalomas, Tel: 76 25 81.

Jeep Safaris: Safaris in open jeeps are offered near the go-cart track. Adults pay about £18 ($31), children £15 ($27). Food is included in the price.

Medical Care

For Maspalomas/San Agustin, Clinica San Agustin, Playa de San Agustin; Tel: 76 27 03 (only for emergencies). Next to the golf course: Centro Medico Maspalomas, Tel: 76 33 92.

Police: Carretera General, Tel: 76 24 18.

Medical Care

Medical care on Gran Canaria is very good and meets most western standards. In the larger cities and tourist centres, there are emergency centres, medical specialists and governmental or private clinics, some of which are under Scandinavian, British or American management. In the smaller cities and villages, if one does not find a hospital then there will always at least be a Red Cross station. "Cruz Roja" is the Spanish term for these stations, which will at the very least be equipped with an ambulance. Red Cross employees can be recognised by a uniform similar to that of a soldier: a green battle uniform with laced black boots. One will also see them on the ferries operating between the islands. The following is a summary of the emergency medical services offered. Additional addresses and telephone numbers can be found under individual entries.

Las Palmas

Emergency Unit (city centre): Paseo Tomas Morales: Tel: 24 51 57, Harbour de la Luz, Tel: 26 44 73

Hospital Insular: Avenida Maritma del Sur; Tel: 31 30 33.

British Hospital, Paseo de la Cornisa, Tel: 25 42 43.

Residencia Sanitaria "Nuestra Señora del Pino," Angel Guimera 87; Tel: 23 11 99. Emergency service for house calls: Tel: 24 66 42. Ambulance, Tel: 24 05 23.

International Clinic, Nuñez de Arce 2; Tel: 24 56 43.

British and American Clinic: Fagasta 5; Tel: 26 45 35.

Playa del Ingles

Medical Centre near "Yumbo Shopping Centre"; Tel: 76 12 92.

British Suomi Clinic, Ed. Buenos Aires (hotel), Tel: 76 27 03.

24-hour service, Dr. Eusebio Caminio Perez, Ed. Iguazu, Tel: 76 48 94.

Dentist Dr. Carlos Maya Caceres, Ed. Excelsior I, Tel: 76 32 80.
Red Cross Station on the beaches of Playa del Ingles and Maspalomas.

Maspalomas/San Agustin
Clinica San Agustin; Tel: 76 27 03 (only emergency service).

Puerto Rico
British American Clinic, Tel: 74 54 47; Medical Consulting, Tel: 74 51 34.

Arucas
Tel: 60 01 65

Telde
Tel: 69 01 35

Medication

Some visitors will find that they react sensitively to the unaccustomed climate
and food. The "Canarian fever" has quite often been the cause for spending
a day in close proximity to certain facilities. In the tourist centres there are
always →*Pharmacies* which have meanwhile adapted to this tourist-specific
problem. Charcoal tablets or laxatives for the opposite problem should be
brought along.

*A striking contrast: the white village church of Mogan against the deep blue
of the sky*

Foot powder will prevent foot fungus. The beaches are not always clean, which is also true for swimming pools and showers. Bandages for minor injuries and iodine will protect against infection, should one be injured on the stones at the beach. The Canary Islands — with the exception of Fuerteventura and Lanzarote — are a veritable paradise for hikers. The paths are, however, quite often slippery and rugged. Elastic bandages will help in case of sprains. Eye drops will be of help to those whose eyes react sensitively to the intense sunlight — especially on the beach. Suntan lotion should also be included in the suit-case. The skin must gradually become accustomed to the sun. Those who ambitiously try to tan quickly will find that the tan peels off just as quickly. The amount of exposure to the sun should be increased very gradually. It is also better to move about in the fresh air than to lie flat on the beach, where the sun is even more intense than inland due to the reflection of the water.
→*Medical Care, Vaccinations, Equipment*

Mirador de Balcon

The observation point Mirador de Balcon offers one of the most breathtaking experiences on Gran Canaria. It is located on the western coast, beneath the Carrizo mountain (514 metres/1,680 feet high) on the road GC 810 between Agaete and Puerto de San Nicolas. Indeed, a small balcony offers the oppor-tunity for a rest high above the vertical drop of the cliffs. It is worthwhile to take time here and enjoy the unobstructed view of the entire northwestern coast.

Mirador de Zamora

The Mirador de Zamora lies between Teror and Valleseco in the northern cen-tral regions of Gran Canaria. This observation point is at an altitude of 900 metres (almost 3,000 feet) from which one can see all the way to Las Palmas and to the coast during clear weather. One does not necessarily need binoculars.

What cannot be overlooked is the Bar-Restaurante "Balcon de Zamora" on the left-hand side toward Valleseco and only 150 metres (165 yards) further to the right is the Bar-Restaurante "Valleseco" and opposite to this, the "Meson Los Roquettes" with an unusual of stones covered in whitewashed cement. The latter is a restaurant with a swimming pool for those with discerning tastes and larger budgets. The "Balcon de Zamora" offers inexpensive fish dishes, simple omelettes priced from 50p (88 cents) and complete meals from £4 ($7). The "Valleseco" is not only geographically between the other two but also in terms of price.

Miraflor

The road number 817 leads from Tamaraceite through a shallow valley by the Presa de Tenoya reservoir via Miraflor to Teror. To the right of the road lined with eucalyptus trees, there are several caves shortly before reaching Miraflor. Growing in the terraced fields are various types of vegetables, oranges and lemons but also prickly pears and agaves.

Mogan

Twelve kilometres (7½ miles) from Puerto de la Cruz, the road number 812 ends in an intersection. Turing left, the street leads to Puerto de Mogan; to the right, after 7 more kilometres (4½ miles) through the egg-plant and banana plantations, through the Barranco de Mogan to the village of Mogan.

About 7,900 people live in the district of Mogan. These people reportedly physically resemble their ancestors from the 15th and 16th centuries, which are considered the archetype of the Canarian shepherd. The clothing of that time is no longer in fashion: shirts made from coarse material and trousers with broad legs cut above the knee, resembling a skirt. In addition to this, a vest was worn for warmth, but to allow for free movement of the arms.

The Red Cross station can be found to the left of the road shortly before entering the town. To the right, the restaurant "Acaymo" is definitely worth visiting, especially during the evening. The fish dishes are highly recommended. There are also three apartments which can be rented. It is best to call ahead: Tel: 56 90 13 / 79. The restaurant is closed Mondays. From the main road, another road branches off to the right, leading up to the centre of town where telephones can also be found.

Mogan / **Practical Information**

Accommodation: There are only very few hotels and holiday accommodations in Mogan.

Apartments "Acaymo" (→*see above*)

"Casa Mina," Tel: 56 90 41, from £9 ($15) for two persons, with a kitchen. This is a small conglomeration of five rooms which make up a small house. When entering the town from the south, one will pass by the restaurant "Acaymo" on the left and after about 100 metres (110 yards) one will see "Casa Mina" on the left. Señora Mina lives in the house next door to the left.

Guest House "Bartolo"*, Lomo Quiebre 32, Tel: 74 04 82, five rooms for about £9 ($15), there is also a bar.

Currency Exchange: Caja Rural, Calle General Franco, next to the town hall.

Post Office: Calle General Franco, next to the town hall.

Restaurants
Restaurant "Acaymo " (→*see above*).
Restaurant "El Alamo," and Bar-Restaurante "El Laurel" are both popular meeting places on the main thoroughfare to San Nicolas de Tolentino.

Money

There are no limits to the amount of foreign currencies allowed to be brought into the country; however, larger amounts which are subsequently bought to the Spanish mainland must be declared upon arrival. Spanish pesetas may also be brought to Gran Canaria in unlimited amounts. Per person, 100.000 pesetas and foreign currencies with a value of up to 500.000 may be taken out without having any questions asked.

Banks are open Monday to Friday from 9 am to 2 pm; on Saturdays to 1 pm. In addition, there are currency exchange offices ("Cambio") and money can also be exchanged at the reception of larger hotels — albeit at a less favourable exchange rate. The official exchange rates are posted in the banks. One can also ask for these in larger hotels.

The focal point of Moya: the Candelaria Church

Eurocheques are accepted. These have the advantage that the amount is not already deducted from a bank account before departing as is the case with traveller's cheques. However, traveller's checks are insured for the entire amount if lost or stolen. In Spain, the fees for cashing Eurocheques are lower than for traveller's cheques.

Montaña de las Cuatro Puertas →*Cuatro Puertas*

Moya

Moya is an unspoiled rural town between Arucas and Guia in the northern part of Gran Canaria. Two small roads lead from here by the caves of Cenobio de Valeron to the northern coast with the fishing villages El Pagador and San Felipe. Moya is situated in a fertile valley. Citrus fruits and numerous eucalyptus and pine trees grow on the extensive plantations.

Life in Moya is focussed predominantly along the Magistral Merrier street. On this street, there are pharmacies, a post office, a public telephone and on the corner of Calle Juan Dialogued in front of the library is a taxi stand. At the end of Magistral Marrero is the Plaza de Candelaria with the Candelaria Church.

In the fertile valley of Moya are, in addition to citrus fruit, pine and eucalyptus forests

The Avenida General Mola leads to an intersection outside of town. The street to the left, the GC 160 leads by the discotheque "El Pilar-La Fonda" and the guest house "El Pilar" heading toward Fontanales. The guest house is presently being renovated, but should be reopened in 1992.

Nudism

Among the local residents of the Canary Islands, nudism is frowned upon. They dress conservatively and also behave as such in public. Still, the Canarians do tolerate it on most beaches when women swim or sunbathe topless — and this at any age.

Therefore, it is left up to the individual traveller how much skin he or she wishes to expose to the intensive rays of the sun. There is, however, a limit to this general rule: on Gran Canaria, people go naked into restaurants, shops and bars just as seldom as in other countries. On the beaches complete nudity is generally not acceptable, and this applies to men as well as women. There are, however, official and unofficial exceptions to this rule: nudism is practised on the beach Playa de los Amadores, for instance, northwest of Puerto Rico shortly before the campsite of Tauro. The footpath leading there is quite a strenuous hike leading over the rocks along the road.

Further options are the secluded bays, set apart from the more heavily frequented beaches. One tip, especially interesting for young people is Güigüi. This beach is only accessible during low tide and one must then plan to sleep outdoors the following night — isolated from the comfort and convenience of restaurants and hotels.

Those who would rather forgo this can find a spot on the beach among the dunes of Maspalomas or on the beach marked off as "Zona Nudista" between Playa del Ingles and Maspalomas. This is the only official nudist beach on the island and watchmen patrol the beaches, making sure that people do not run about naked elsewhere.

Otherwise, nudists should note: as long as passers-by do not wrinkle their nose in disgust, nude bathing is probably not disturbing anyone. The more secluded the area, the "less" is possible.

One should, however, respect the Spanish sense of modesty and not be more outgoing than the Spaniards themselves — and by no means in their presence. Otherwise, it could come to the same result as in the south of Fuerteventura, where the government hires watchmen to patrol the beaches. Offences against public order are prosecuted — and nude bathing falls under this category.

Oasis →*Maspalomas*
Palmitos Park →*Maspalomas*

Parador Nacional Cruz de Tejeda

The government run hotel at Cruz de Tejeda lies at an altitude 1,450 metres (4,741 feet) above sea level on a mountain ridge. During good weather, one can see Roque Bentaiga and Roque Nublo as well as the snow covered summit of Pico de Teide on Tenerife. Cruz de Tejeda is, however, described as a "petrified storm" since it is sooner foggy, damp and cold here. From here, one can also hike through the beautiful, old pine forests of Tamadaba.

The Parador Nacional Cruz de Tejeda is a restaurant. Formerly, it was also a hotel. However, this portion is being renovated and will probably not reopen before 1995. Tel: 65 80 50, Fax: 65 80 51.

Parque Ornitologico →*Maspalomas*
Parque Santa Catalina →*Las Palmas*

Pharmacies

Pharmacies ("farmacias") display a green or red Maltese cross. Those who have brought along a specific medication that cannot be purchased on Gran Canaria should present the slip included in the packaging. This way, the pharmacist can at least identify a similar medication. Pharmacies on Gran Canaria are generally well stocked. When purchasing prescription medication, one should request a receipt so that one is reimbursed by one's health insurance company upon returning home.

Photography

The same film and supplies are available on Gran Canaria as are common in other western countries. This is especially true in the larger cities and holiday centres. Prices are also comparable. Film can be developed on the Canary Islands. One day or even one-hour developing service is available almost everywhere. The quality is generally good.

Travellers who would rather have their film developed at home need not worry about the x-rays during security checks at the airports. Baggage is x-rayed, but this will not damage the film. Those who have reservations about film with a light sensitivity over 1000 ASA can request that the security officials check through the baggage by hand.

It is always a question of tact when taking pictures of the local people. It can never hut to ask courteously — and a banana farmer who has just harvested a 200 pound stem of Chinese Cavendish bananas will be just as proud to have his picture taken next to it as would a fisherman with his prize-winning catch.

Pico de Bandama →*Caldera de Bandama*

Pinar de Tamadaba

From Cruz de Tejeda, the road GC 110 leads via Artenara to the pine forests of Pinar de Tamadaba. From Artenara, it is another 12 kilometres (7½ miles) to the summit of Las Presas, around which the road winds. From here it should be possible to see the northwestern coast of the island, and this would be the case if the tall Canarian pines did not obstruct the view to the ocean.

Playa de la Aldea →*Puerto de San Nicolas*

Playa del Ingles

Playa del Ingles is a beach measuring 6 kilometres (4 miles) composed of fine sand and dunes. It is located between Maspalomas and San Agustin in the southern region of Gran Canaria. This is the reason that Playa del Ingles has developed into one of the largest tourist centres on the Canary Islands. Entertainment is offered around the clock. This tourist centre is overwhelming. It is the number one focus of tourism on the island. In many of the hotels there are discotheques, or dances are organised outdoors. The Avenida de Tirajana, 1.2 kilometres (three quarters of a mile) from the beach, has everything that a tourist's heart could desire: shopping centres, supermarkets, cafés and bars line the street. In addition, there are the larger shopping centres like "Cita, "Kasbah" and "Chapparal." Finding something typically Canarian or rooted in the Canarian culture is a sheer impossibility. Those hoping for a quiet, relaxing holiday should best give Playa del Ingles a wide berth.

On the beach, strict rules must be observed. These are enforced by patrolmen. Also, large signs make visitors aware of the fact that camping, campfires and music are not allowed on the beach. Dogs are not welcome either.

Playa del Ingles / **Practical Information**
Accommodation

In comparison to the accommodation in Maspalomas, Playa del ingles is usually booked as part of a package tour, and the number of vacant hotel rooms is limited. It is mainly the expensive hotels, which will have vacancies, but this is quite an expensive option.

The extensive pine forests colour the volcanic islands of Gran Canaria with shades of green ▶

Hotel "Catarina Playa"****, Avenida de Tirajana 1, Tel: 76 28 12, 402 rooms, between £40 ($71) and £90 ($159).

Hotel "Don Gregory"****, Las Tabaibas 11, Tel: 76 26 58. 241 rooms, between £94 ($165) and £140 ($247).

Hotel "Buenaventura Playa"***, Plaza Ansite s/n., Tel: 76 16 50. 716 rooms, between £34 ($59) and £77 ($136).

Hotel Residencia "Continental"***, Avenida de Italia 2, Tel: 76 00 33. 383 rooms, around £50 ($89).

Hotel "Eugenia Victoria"***, Avenida de Gran Canaria 26, Tel: 76 25 00. 400 rooms, between £40 ($71) and £60 ($106).

Hotel "Playa del Ingles"***, Avenida de Italia 27, Tel: 76 08 00. 189 rooms, between £ 24 ($42) and £30 ($53).

Hotel "Escorial"**, Avenida de Italia 6, Tel: 76 13 58. 251 rooms, £34 ($59).

Hotel "Rondo"**, Avenida de Tirajana 38, Tel: 76 05 20. 101 rooms, between £30 ($53) and £44 ($77).

Bungalow "Biarritz" (three keys), Avenida de Bonn 18, Tel: 76 16 12. Apartments from £29 ($52) for three persons to £40 ($70) for five persons.

Apartments "Amazonas" (two keys), Marruecos 4, Tel: 76 18 38. 96 apartments each for three persons at £40 ($71).

Apartments "Dertusa I" and "Dertusa II" (one key), Avenida de Alemania 19. A total of 18 apartments, each for three persons, from £25 ($44).

Apartments "Mirasol" (one key), Avenida Marruecos 5, Tel: 76 12 71. 35 apartments between £17 ($30) and £27 ($47).

Car Rental

The car rental agency "Magi" has specialised in the rental of old-timers. These old cars, however have been refurbished with powerful Citroën engines. Avenida de Tirajana, Edificio Barbados I, Tel: 76 27 31.

Other car rental agencies:

"Autos Europa," Edificio Barbados, Tel: 76 04 83.

"Marosa," Avenida de Tirajana 29, Tel: 76 54 90 and 76 54 94; Avenida de Galdar s/n., Tel: 76 70 54 and 76 70 58.

"Atesa," Avenida de Tirajana 22, Tel: 76 51 99, 76 52 91 and 76 50 93.

"Cicar," Avenida de Alemania 10, Tel: 76 15 34, 76 15 35; Edificio Las Walkiras, Avenida Alfereces Prov., Tel: 76 18 57 and 76 03 51.

"Avis," Centro Commercial El Veril, Tel: 76 09 63; Edificio Bayuca — Alfereces Provisionales 35, Tel: 76 54 26 and 76 54 27.

"Occa," Hotel "E. Victoria," Tel: 76 13 39 and 76 04 77; V. Insular Maspalomas, Tel: 76 05 00 and 76 20 50; V. Insular Maritim, Tel: 76 13 67 and 56 20 50.

"Hertz," Avenida de Italia s/n., (Hotel "Continental"), Tel: 76 25 72 and 76 25 83.

"Cita," c/o Viajes Cita, El Veril, Local 16, Tel: 76 30 21 and 76 79 66; Avenida de Francia, Tel: 76 40 92 and 76 42 70.

"Orlando," Avenida de Tirajana 23, Tel: 76 24 85; Avenida de Gran Canaria 14, Tel: 76 43 66 and Avenida de Tenerife 3, Tel: 76 14 23.

Medical Care

Medical Centre near "Yumbo Shopping Centre," Tel: 76 12 92.

British Suomi Clinic, Ed. Buenos Aires (hotel), Tel: 76 27 03.

24-hour service, Dr. Eusebio Caminio Perez, Ed. Iguazu, Tel: 76 48 94.

Dentist Dr. Carlos Maya Caceres, Ed. Excelsior I, Tel: 76 32 80.

Red Cross Station on the beaches of Playa del Ingles and Maspalomas.

Post Office: Avenida de Tirajana, Edificio Mercurio, open from 9 am to 1 pm.

Shopping: In the shopping centres "Cita," "La Sandia," "Kasbah," and "Yumbo" are, in addition to discotheques and nightclubs and restaurants, numerous shops, supermarkets and newsstands.

Important Addresses and Tips

Iberia/Trasmediterranea: "Viajes Canyrama," Edificio Mercurio, Tel: 76 13 41 and 76 18 34.

Beach Chairs and Umbrellas: The licences for renting out the beach chairs and umbrellas are newly awarded regularly. Therefore, the prices can vary. As an orientation, chairs and umbrellas for two people should cost no more than £7 ($12) per day.

Paddle-boats: These can be rented on the beach for about £5 ($9).

Playa del Tauro →*Tauro*
Playa de San Agustin →*San Agustin*

Police

There are three types of police in Spain and also on the Canary Island: the "Policia Municipal" (dark brown uniforms) has the function to maintain order and is concerned mainly with traffic violations. The "Guardia Civil" (green uniforms) is responsible for emergencies, for instance when reporting a theft. The emergency telephone numbers are posted in every telephone booth. The hotel reception will be able to help if there is a problem with the language. Remaining to be mentioned is the "General de Policia" which is responsible for felonies.

Politics

Politically, this archipelagos has been a part of Spain since being conquered in the 15th century. Today, the administration is divided into two provinces;

Las Palmas de Gran Canaria with Las Palmas de Gran Canaria as its capital
is comprised of the islands of Gran Canaria, Fuerteventura, Lanzarote and
the Isletas (→*Geography*).

Santa Cruz de Tenerife is the second province with Santa Cruz de Tenerife
as its capital and including the islands of Tenerife, La Palma, El Hierro and
La Gomera.

On each of the islands, there is a "Cabildos Insulares" the independent insular administration.

In recent decades, the Canary Islands have witnessed the development of
political groups who call for the independence of the archipelagos. This is
more or less an academic discussion; it is not likely that Spain will give up
the control of these islands.

Population and People

The total population of the Canary Islands is estimated at 1.5 million to date.
In 1980, 50,000 lived on Lanzarote; 19,000 on Fuerteventura; 630,000 on Gran
Canaria; 610,000 on Tenerife, 24,000 on La Gomera, 6,000 on El Hierro and
81,000 on La Palma.

Dominoes are extremely popular on all of the Canary Islands

The number of tourists outnumbers that of the residents by far, which has a notable effect on the water supply.

Each island has its own character and is thus heavily influenced by its residents. **Lanzarote** is flat, hot, the landscape formed by hard-working farmers and architects. The fields always appear well tended due to a special method of farming *(→Economy)*. The residents live mainly from agriculture; tourism is limited to only a few areas.

Fuerteventura is for fishermen; agriculture has been neglected and has missed the opportunity of which for instance Lanzarote has taken advantage. The island is untamed, craggy and has long sandy beaches along its coast, which attract visitors from all over the world.

Gran Canaria has the entire spectrum of landscapes: mountains, beaches and forests. The island is just as suited to agriculture as it is to fishermen and shepherds — and tourists. The same is true for **Tenerife.** Both of these, the largest islands of the Canaries, have absorbed the flood of tourism without losing their own character.

La Palma has only begun to become accustomed to the numerous visitors. When the international airport was opened in 1987, protest arose, directed toward the tourists who would now start to arrive. However, tourism would bring money — and foreigners were already there: the selling out of the island had begun much earlier. Many landowners do not even make the effort to find Spanish buyers for their land. On signs posted in fields showing the owner's willingness to sell, "for sale" or "zu verkaufen" takes the place of "se vende." For this as well as other reasons, especially older residents fear being overrun.

El Hierro and **La Gomera** are the most untamed, untouched and demanding of the Canary Islands. Those visiting these islands will have to adapt to the cold as well as the heat, to high as well as low humidity — and this separated only by a few miles. On La Gomera, it is only the Valle Gran Rey, the valley of the great kings, which has suffered from tourism. That which began as an alternative to the tourist centres is now leading to a questionable counter-culture with which only the most thick-skinned and entrepreneurial Canarians can cope: the prices are hardly any longer acceptable for the residents because in the past years, they have doubled or even tripled. Without respect for the natives, tourists swim naked and smoke questionable substances — quite unpleasant for the conservative residents. An assimilation or even an understanding between the young travellers and the residents of Valle Gran Rey has not taken place. The visitors have brought with them a culture which they were not able to realise in their own country — and force it on their hosts. The inhabitants of the Canary Islands are hospitable as were their ancestors the Guanches. And of them, it is also said that they were hard-working, honest and enjoyed music, dancing and life. They met the challenge set forth by their environment which was often hostile. And so it remains today.

Postal System

Post offices are open Monday to Friday from 9 am to 1 pm and some reopen from 5 to 7 pm. Postage stamps can also be purchased in the "estancos," the tobacco shops, and at many of the hotel reception desks. They can also be purchased when buying postcards.

Letters of up to 20 grams and postcards sent to EC member states 45 Pesetas; to other countries within Europe, these cost 55 Pesetas. There is no extra fee for airmail delivery within Europe. Those who would like to have letters, parcels or money sent to them can do this by general delivery: "en lista de correos." One must ask for the exact address of the post office.

Mail boxes for normal deliveries are yellow with two horizontal red stripes. The ones for express deliveries are red.

Prices →*Shopping*
Pueblo Sioux →*Sioux City*
Puerto de la Luz →*Las Palmas*

Puerto de las Nieves

The small harbour of Puerto de las Nieves, in the coastal region of Punta de la Aldea de San Nicolas near Agaete in Gran Canaria's northwest, is situated on a protected, shallow bay which is bordered on one side by basalt cliffs crowned with pine trees. The famous Dedo de Dios, the finger of God, reaches out of the ocean beyond these natural walls. Like a giant index finger, this monolith towers 30 metres (98 feet). Plans have already been made to expand the harbour into a yacht harbour.

The village church is named "Virgen de las Nieves." The statue of Mary and a three-panelled, Flemish alter from the 16th century are visited every year on August fifth by thousands of pious pilgrims.

When coming from San Nicolas de Tolentino, one must turn left of the road number 819 before Agaete and head toward Puerto de las Nieves. There are two service stations on the main thoroughfare.

Shortly before reaching the promenade in Puerto de las Nieves, not far from the old, run-down windmill on Avenida Las Poetas, one can eat quite inexpensively at the "La Granja" restaurant, especially fish. Additional restaurants are located on the Plaza (Bar-Restaurante "Capita") and along the harbour, with a view of the finger of God, "Dedo de Dios" or "Vistamar" directly on the beach promenade

Accommodation

Most of the restaurants also rent out apartments, although not for under three days. Prices: from £13.50 ($23.50) per night.

Puerto de Mogan

Road number 812 ends 12 kilometres (7½ miles) northwest of Puerto Rico at the canyon Barranco de Mogan. To the right, the street continues as GC 810 to Mogan; branching left, it leads past a large nursery and papaya plantation to the fishing village of Puerto de Mogan, in which tourism has gradually begun to set root. The town is picturesque and practically unspoiled, even though the beach Playa de Mogan on the lovely bay is packed with sunbathers. Puerto de Mogan can still be considered beyond the beaten tourist track in the southern region of the island.

Puerto de Mogan / **Practical Information**

Accommodation: Along the road leading off to Puerto de Mogan, there is a newer and well kept, family operated guest house. Apartments are also available here.

Guest House "Eva," Tel: 74 00 86. Apartments include a kitchenette and bath and cost £9 ($15) for two persons, but is somewhat untidy.

Guest House "Magali," Tel: 74 03 41, £9 ($15) for two person including a kitchenette, very clean, light guest house.

Guest House "Lucrecia," Tel: 74 02 28, £9 ($15) for two persons. Spacious, light rooms which share a kitchen. Very clean, friendly proprietor.

Guest House "Lumy," Tel: 74 01 71, £9 ($15). Located on a mountain, includes a kitchenette. The family's terrace can also be used by guests.

Guest House "Salvadore," Tel: 74 01 89. This family operated guest house is located in the centre of town. A double room costs £11 ($20) and includes a kitchenette. Because the guest house is somewhat hidden in a small alleyway, it is best to ask directions in the "Salvadore" bar. When entering the town, this can be found on the right-hand side of the street beyond the last bridge but before the traffic circle.

Hotel "Club de Mar"***, Tel: 74 01 00, Fax: 74 02 23, double rooms from £30 ($53), apartments from £37 ($65).

Guest House "Bartolome," apartment for two persons with kitchen and bath for £7 ($12).

Aparthotel "Revoli"****, Avenida de Mogan s/n., Tel: 74 50 01. 181 rooms, up to £64 ($112).

Hotel "Puerto Plata"***, Avenida de la Cornisa s/n., Tel: 74 51 50. 246 rooms, between £13.50 ($24) and £24 ($42).

Apartments "Aruba" (two keys), Avenida de Mogan Puerto Rico, Tel: 74 50 67. 16 apartments between £11 ($19) and £14 ($25).

Apartments "Cavay" (two keys), Avenida Mogan 32, Tel: 74 57 35. 18 apartments, from £25 ($45).

Apartments "La Fontana" (one key), Avenida Ancla 12, Tel: 74 60 45. 8 apartments, between £13.50 ($24) and £19 ($33).

Apartments "Mogan" (one key), Calle de las Conchas 6 and 8, Tel: 74 03 57. 6 apartments from £15 ($27) to £20 ($36).

Car Rental: "Atesa Rent a Car," Hotel "Club de Mar," Tel: 74 01 00.

Autos "Abrahama," Tel: 74 02 65. A Seat Marbella costs around £17 ($30) per day, including insurance.

Puerto de San Nicolas

The pier of the quaint fishing village of Puerto de San Nicolas, west of San Nicolas de Tolentino attracts fishermen mainly during the evening hours. By this time, the swimmers and sunbathers have left the beach. Directly along the harbour where the fishermen repair their nets and touch up the paint on their boats, there are various bars and restaurants, for example, "Luis," "Aquas Marina" and "Mirador Touristico El Charco." In these restaurants, one can order the fish that were brought on land in the morning. It can't get much fresher than this — or less expensive. Meals cost from £3.50 ($6) to £5 ($9).

The road from San Nicolas de Tolentino to Puerto de San Nicolas and continuing to Agaete, leads through a dry, dusty valley, in which scattered windmills produce electricity or pump the precious commodity of water from the ground. The population of this small harbour town lives mainly from fishing; some resident make their living in the distillery "San Nicolas."

Puerto de Sardina → *Sardina*

Puerto Rico

In the young city of Puerto Rico, originally a fishing harbour, hardly nothing remains of the original flair. For aquatic sportsmen and disco hoppers it is *the*

Like a huge index finger the "Dedo de Dios," the finger of God, towers above a bay ▶

city on Gran Canaria. However, it also has bowling centres and squash courts for those who would like to keep fit during their holidays without getting their feet wet. Otherwise, Puerto Rico and the neighbouring towns consist predominantly of hotels, stores and bazaars.

Each beach can be distinguished by the colour of the beach chairs which are set up each morning, weather permitting — and it usually does.

The harbour of Puerto Rico can accommodate over 100 yachts and fishing boats. During the late afternoon hours, the sports fishermen return and present their catch.

Puerto Rico / **Practical Information**
Accommodation

Apartments "Rio Piedras" (three keys), Avenida del Ancla 2, Tel: 74 58 98. 98 apartments, between £34 ($59) and £77 ($136).

Apartments "Barbados 1" and "Barbados 2" (two keys), Avenida Rio Piedras, Tel: 74 52 29. 17 apartments, between £16 ($29) and £21 ($37).

Apartments "Puerto Bello" (one key), Calle Tasartico s/n., Tel: 74 52 52. 57 apartments between £13.50 ($24) and £18 ($31).

Car Rental: "Cita," c/o Viajes Cita, near the British-American Clinic, Tel: 74 57 33.

"Cicar," Complex Orinoco, Tel: 74 57 17.

"Orlando," Centro Civico Comercial, Tel: 74 59 79; Complejo Apartementos Panama, Tel: 74 52 96.

"Occa," Aparthotel "Greco," Tel: 74 53 46.

Currency Exchange: It is best to go to the shopping centre where various banks are located. To get to the shopping centre, one must continue along the thoroughfare and turn left at the traffic circle when coming form the west.

Medical Care: British-American Clinic, Tel: 74 57 47; Medical Consulting Tel: 74 51 34.

Religion

Spain is a predominantly Catholic country. The majority of the residents of the Canary Islands are also Catholic.

Reptilandia →*Sardina*

Restaurants

Food and drink are served in the "bars" and the "restaurantes." In this guide, they are referred to as "bar-restaurantes." In the bar "tapas" are usually served.

These are small snacks for between meals, costing up to about £2 ($3.50). The bars also serve different types of coffee: black, coffee with milk espresso or coffee with a shot of liqueur or Cognac. Most bars open at 9 am at the latest because this is when the working class eats breakfast. Women can only rarely be seen in the bars, although they are not officially unwelcome.

Lunch or dinner in the restaurants cost from £5 ($9) to £7 ($12) including an appetiser, a main course, dessert and a beverage. Water is served with every meal upon request: normal drinking water ("agua sin gas") is not always added to the bill; mineral water ("agua con gas"), on the other hand, always is charged extra. It is served in large bottles.

Bread is a part of every meal. Sometimes an extra charge for bread is added to the bill. If this happens, one should definitely complain to the management if the price is unreasonable.

→*also individual entries*

Risco →*El Risco*

Roque Bentaiga

The holy mountain of the Guanches, the Roque Bentaiga, can best be seen from Artenara. It is 1,404 metres (4,591 feet) high.

Roque Nublo

This is a paradise for hikers. The Roque Nublo is in the island's centre, reaching an elevation of 1,803 (5,896 feet). On the summit, a monolith towers 80 metres (260 feet). Beneath it are prickly pears and dragon trees.

San Agustin

In comparison to Playa del Ingles, San Agustin is more compact, located in a landscape of sand dunes. The hotel complexes can be found in the oasis. San Agustin is foremost a tourist centre on an interesting section of coastline, with dark sand and bizarre cliff formations. The residents here number a little over 1,000. Due to the number of tourists on the southern coast of Gran Canaria, the population has multiplied in the past years.

It is only 5 kilometres (3 miles) to the entertainment centres in Playa del Ingles; there is also a bus line operating to Playa del Ingles. The Casino is also in San Agustin, accepting bets between 250 and 100,000 pesetas, offering French and American roulette, punto y banca, craps and black jack as well as slot machines. The casino, in the Tamarindos hotel, is open from 9 pm to 4 am. One must also bring a passport or identity card.

San Agustin / **Practical Information**
Accommodation

Hotel "Tamarindos"*****, Retama 3, Tel: 76 20 00. 318 rooms, between £110 ($195) and £150 ($265).

Hotel "Ifa Beach,"***, Los Jazmines 25, Tel: 76 51 99. 200 rooms, priced at £50 ($89) and £59 ($103).

Car Rental: "Maroso," Retama 5, Tel: 76 06 82.

"Occa," Bungalows Rocas Rojas, Tel: 76 59 41.

"Orlando," Centro Commercial San Agustin, Tel: 76 42 16; Urbanizacion Bahia Feliz, Tel: 76 34 07.

Casino: Casino Tamarindos S.A., C/. Las Retamas 3, San Agustin, Tel: 76 27 24.

Entertainment

There is a sport centre near the "Inter Club Atlantic." Here, one can jump on the trampoline, play shuffleboard and table tennis or try one's hand at wind surfing if the wind is right.

One of the most significant entertainment centres is the "Cita" with the "Scala" (Tel: 76 68 28 and 76 68 34). This night club prides itself on the "unforgettable evening" that guests can experience here.

Medical Care: Clinica San Agustin, Playa San Agustin, Tel: 76 27 03 (only emergency service). Dr. Jochen Langhoff, general practitioner, Tel: 76 62 29.

San Bartolome de Tirajana

The city of San Bartolome de Tirajana, at an altitude of 850 metres (2,780 feet), is located west of Santa Lucia and south of the Pico de las Nieves in a huge depression in the central mountain range. Shortened, the name of the town is merely San Bartolome, but its complete name comes from th canyon Barranco de Tirajana, which runs through the city.

San Bartolome is accessible by the road number 815 via Agüimes. or, when coming from the north, on the road number 811 from Cruz de Tejeda.

The church in the centre of town dates back to the 17th century, built long after the island was conquered by the Spanish. The Spaniard Pedro de Vera occupied the villages so long that the Guanches surrendered. At that time, the island lost the original name of Tamaran and has been called Gran Canaria ever since.

San Bartolome / **Practical Information**
Bus Stop: Calle Reyes Catholicos.
Currency Exchange: Caja Rural, Calle Reyes Catholicos.

Restaurants

There are various restaurants and bars in San Bartolome. The "Castillo del San Bartolome," on the Road to Fataga, offers guests an original atmosphere (Carretera Fataga 560, Tel: 79 82 25). In a stylish, knightly dining hall, visitors can dine as the armour-clad warriors one did long ago. The Castillo is especially recommended for breakfast, priced from less than £1.70 ($3).

In two of the bars, rooms are available. Both are located on the left hand side of the main street when coming from Fataga:

Bar "Cuatra Esquinas," Tel: 79 80 84, 1 single and one double room, with a sitting room and kitchen. Small but pleasant. £3.50 ($6) per person. Señora Hustina Perez Monzon scrutinises her guests quite thoroughly. She doesn't accept just anyone because the rooms are decorated with affection.

Bar "Santana Lopez," Tel: 79 81 72. Very simply furnished. Price: £7 ($12) for a room with two beds; also available for one person.

Taxi: Calle Reyes Catholicos.

San Lorenzo

The village of San Lorenzo with its winding alleyways is best explored on foot or with a compact car. A Mercedes limousine would make navigating the inner city of San Lorenzo almost impossible. It is best to park the car on the large Plaza to the right of the main thoroughfare near the "San Lorenzo" bar or the "Rivero" bar, continuing on foot into town.

To get to San Lorenzo, one must drive from Las Palmas via Tamaraceite on the GC 200, and then continue south. A second option is to take road number 812 to Tafira and then turn right onto Jardin Canario and the left after another 3 kilometres (a little under 2 miles) to San Lorenzo. In this town, the huge laurel tree, overshadowing the entire Plaza, is especially worth seeing. There is also a pharmacy and a doctor's office on the Plaza.

San Mateo

San Mateo, also called Vega de San Mateo, is situated southwest of Santa Brigida. This town is particularly well known for its livestock and vegetable market every Sunday, attracting visitors from near and far. San Mateo is also a centre for growing fruit on Gran Canaria. Traffic jams develop at quite a distance outside of town on Sundays, the few bars and restaurants do a great deal of business, and enterprising youths charge thankful visitors a few pesetas to use their fathers' gardens as a parking area. The only spot where it is relatively peaceful is under the laurel trees across from the Almada Santa Ana Church. Finding one's way to the market is not difficult: take the main street and follow the noise and smell of livestock. The source of the noise and distinct aroma is the market.

Currency Exchange: Caja Rural, Carretera General.

Restaurants and Bars: Bar/Cafetería "Mallow" and Pizzeria "Eminentia" are both on the Carretera General.

Service Station: Shortly before leaving the city, toward Las Lagunetas and Cruz de Tejeda.

San Nicolas de Tolentino

San Nicolas de Tolentino lies at the tip of a canyon, measuring 5 kilometres (3¼ miles) in length, which leads to →*Puerto San Nicolas* on the coast at the Playa de la Aldea. San Nicolas de Tolentino is the largest city in the western region of Gran Canaria with a population, which is on the average younger than in cities on the eastern side of the island. The city also serves as a shopping centre for the region.

There are signs along the narrow, but well paved road for the "Presas," the reservoirs. Thanks to them and the windmills which pump water from the ground, San Nicolas de Tolentino enjoys relative affluence. The windmills are necessary being that the reservoirs do dry up during some months.

San Nicolas de Tolentino / **Practical Information**

Accommodation: One accommodation which is recommended is the guest house "Carmelo" near the "Carmelo" bar on Calle General Franco 83. The proprietor and owner of the guest house also owns the adjacent garage. He rents out five double rooms without breakfast for £7.75 ($13.50) and can be contacted by phoning Tel: 89 09 45.

Secondly, the Bar/Guest House "Legundo" can also be recommended. It is somewhat more expensive, with a double room priced at £11 (19.50). It is located next to the church.

Currency Exchange: Caja Rural on Calle Cervantes.

Entertainment: The young people of San Nicolas meet in the "Alameda" discotheque on Calle General Franco. It is a unpretentious discotheque which keeps up with the newest musical trends. It gets most animated here during weekends.

Medical Care: About 1¼ miles to the north of San Nicolas de Tolentino is the Red Cross Station, offering first aid in emergencies.

Service Stations: Located in the centre of town and outside of town toward Puerto de San Nicolas across from the "Faustio" restaurant.

San Pedro

The village of San Pedro lies between Agaete and the Embalse de los Perez in the north of Gran Canaria. It seems to hang on the walls of a narrow, lush valley. Oranges, lemons and papayas grow in this valley, as do dates; in the higher altitudes, pine trees. Drinking water is bottled above the village of San Pedro at the Berranzales spring. This water is almost as famous as the drinking water from Firgas, which can be purchased on all of the Canary Islands. The Hotel "Princesa Guayarmina" was built on the road to the spring and reservoir. The rear portion of the hotel looks somewhat run down. Inside, however, it is tastefully decorated with antique furnishings. The "Princesa "Guayarmina" is also a health resort, located far enough from the tourist centres that a relaxing walk through the mountains is possible. It is owned by the Suarez family, who make every effort to serve their guests only natural foods. Traditional Canarian cuisine is also emphasised. The hotel is equipped with a swimming pool. Prices: single room, £12 ($21); double room with/without bath, £19 ($33.50)/£17.70 ($31); breakfast, £2 ($3.50); lunch or dinner, £5.70 ($10). Reservations can be made by contacting Tel: 89 80 09 or Fax: 89 85 25.

Santa Brigida

Santa Brigida is a city with a number of villas, located southwest of Las Palmas and accessible by the GC 811 on the way to Cruz de Tejeda. The town was built on the rim of a canyon where an abundance grows. The original name of Santa Brigida was "Sataute," alluding to the extensive palm forests that once grew here.
The grapes for the island's best red wines also grow in the regions surrounding Santa Brigida. The wine is called Vino del Monte and was already in production in the city's wine cellars during the colonial period. There are still remnants of the old wine cellars in Santa Brigida.
During the weekend, there are traffic jams outside of town because of those visiting the livestock market in San Mateo, about 4 miles from Santa Brigida. Beyond town, on the right-hand side of the road is the "Rodriguez" bar and to the left, the "Tenderete" bar. A service station can be found on the left-hand side of the road to San Mateo shortly before leaving town.

Santa Lucia

Santa Lucia, southeast of San Bartolome de Tirajana, can be reached via the GC 815. If one continues on this road into town, one will see the Bar-Restaurant "Mirador Santa Lucia" to the right of the road after entering town. This restaurant is used as a discotheque during the evening. Across from this, is the "An-

Puerto de Sardina has two beaches: a smaller, sandy beach and a sand and gravel beach.

The northwestern landmark of Gran Canaria is the Faro de Sardina on Punta Sardina. Those who take the GC 140 to Galdar should follow the signs, turning left up a partially paved, partially gravel road leading to the lighthouse. Construction has been underway here since the mid 1980's. A new tourist centre is planned here, which is supposed to attract not only Spaniards, but also foreign visitors.

Shopping

No one can conclusively say when the actual business hours for stores are. One must try one's luck — the best times are Monday to Friday from 9 am to 1 pm and from 4 to 7 or 8 pm; Saturdays from 9 am to 1 pm. During the Siesta between 1 and 4 pm, nothing much takes place — even some of the churches close during this time.

"Calados," the filigree needlework is not only available on Tenerife. This is, along with baskets and leather goods, a typical souvenir from the islands. "Toledo" crafts — inlaid metal — are also very lovely, but not always authentic. That which feels smooth rather than rough is most likely plastic.

"Made in Cuba" on rum bottles and cigarillos does not always mean that this is true. The local products are sometimes "upgraded" in this way; however, their quality is still quite respectable.

On the beaches, peddlers sell "authentic gold Swiss watches." However, even within the free-trade zone of the Canary islands, gold and jewels are not free. Reputable shops in the larger cities may be somewhat more expensive, but purchasing jewellry here will prevent disappointments later. "Authentic Guanche weapons" are usually neither authentic nor are they good imitations. These are usually copies of fake "originals."

Alcohol, perfume, and tobacco products are inexpensive on the islands because they are duty-free. One is well advised to buy these articles before the return flight because the duty-free shops in the airports — if there are any at all — are usually more expensive than the shops in the cities. Duty-free items purchased aboard the airplane will definitely be more expensive than on the Canaries.

There are numerous shops for those who choose to cook for themselves. Supermarkets will have everything that is available in central Europe, even though these items will be more expensive.

Bargains can be found in the unpretentious shops in the small towns outside of the tourist centres. There, one can buy the basic foods, figs, wine etc. for up to 50% less than in the cities.

Ship Travel → *Travelling to Gran Canaria, Travel on Gran Canaria*

Sights

Gran Canaria would not attract almost two million tourists annually if it did not have a great deal of extras to offer. Among these is quite definitely the climate, which brings the island spring and summer temperatures during the entire year.

One geological attraction is the diverse landscape, beginning with the long, sandy beaches in the south near La Caleta and Puerto de Mogan. The most famous of Gran Canaria's beaches are the dunes of Maspalomas, one of the largest holiday centres on the Canary Islands. Here, one can find bird sanctuaries and amusement parks; shops, bazaars, discotheques and car rental agencies. Those who find spending a holiday in the south too strenuous can hike through the pine forests of Tamadaba or enjoy the magnificent view over the central mountain range in the Cruz de Tejeda region. In this part of the island, the canyons, with their monoliths have been nicknamed the "Colorado" and the "Grand Canyon" of the Canaries. One of the most beautiful vistas in this area is from La Atalaya.

Those who prefer culture to nature will also get their money's worth. Cuatro Puertas, Cenobio de Valeron and the Cueva de las Cruces, the largest network of caves on the Canary Islands, are reminiscent of the Guanche culture. What has remained intact is, for the most part, displayed in the Museo Canario in Las Palmas: mummies, pottery, terracota, weapons, tools. Las Palmas de Gran Canaria is not only the capital of the island, it is also a cultural centre. What Venice Beach and Malibu are to the residents of Las Angeles, Playa del Canteras is to Las Palmas. The beach, measuring 200 metres (954 feet) in width and 3 kilometres (almost 2 miles) in length, has a promenade with countless shops, bazaars, restaurants, discotheques and night clubs. There is also a diverse selection of museums and parks in Las Palmas, in which one can observe the colourful activity.

The churches of Gran Canaria are also worth seeing. Santa Ana in Las Palmas is only one example. Other outstanding churches from the period of the conquest can be found in Teror, Arucas, Telde, Ingenio and Agüimes. Arucas, Galdar and Agaete are also centres for agriculture with huge plantations and fertile valleys yielding oranges, papayas and lemons — even apples, mangoes and coffee.

Sioux City

In Sioux City, the wild west comes to life. Taking the main road from Las Palmas to Maspalomas, another road leads off to the right shortly beyond the Areoclub de Gran Canaria. It leads into the canyon Barranco de Aguila and into a world of cowboys and Indians.

The old west city, called Pueblo Sioux in Spanish, makes an effort to compete with the tinsel towns in the United States and Europe. Aiding in this are the church, the cemetery, the sheriff's building including a jail, stables and padlocks. There are even herds of cattle which are driven through the main street during the shows at noon and 6 pm daily. The bank is robbed; a stunt man is hanged — every occupation has its drawbacks. The art of acting is being prepared for the next show when the noosed is cut saving the stunt man's neck. Sioux City is open from 10 am to 8 pm, admission is £5 ($9), children pay half. In the saloon, the "Western Inn Bar," food is served, and one can even ride one of the mustangs.

Speed Limits

On motorways 120 kmph, on thoroughfares 100 kmph and on two-lane country roads 90 kmph are permitted. Within towns and cities, 50 kmph is permitted as long as there is no sign stating otherwise. Cars towing trailers may not exceed 70 kmph, on motorways 80 kmph and on thoroughfares 110 kmph. On many roads, due to the poor road conditions, one will not be able to drive much faster than an average speed of 35 kmph: the smaller roads are usually unpaved and are not secured at the curves (→ Traffic Regulations, Travel on Gran Canaria).

Sports

The Canary Islands are a virtual paradise for sailing, surfing and hiking. Fishing is also possible, and along the harbours, deep-sea fishing tours are offered — shark fishing, for instance.

Tennis has become quite popular on the island. Tourist centres are equipped with tennis courts and offer tennis lessons. Individual hotels often allow only club members to use their tennis facilities. However, one can become a club member for a limited amount of time, or be invited as a guest by a club member.

Tafira

Tafira is subdivided into an upper city, Tafira Alta, and a lower city, Tafira Baja, which are connected to each other by the road GC 811. Tafira is located southwest of Las Palmas. The Caldera de Bandama are not far, making recreation available to the residents of this city in one of the more beautiful wooded area of the island.

Due to their close proximity to the capital of Las Palmas and their relatively quiet location, Tafira Alta and Tafira Baja have become a more exclusive neighbourhood for those who have made their fortunes in Las Palmas: doctors, businessmen, hotel owners and lawyers have settled here.

Accommodation: Hotel "Los Frailes"*, Carretera del Centro km 8, Tel: 35 12 06. 26 rooms, from £9 ($15). This hotel is more or less a student dormitory. Only very few rooms are kept vacant for other guests.

Tamadaba →*Pinar de Tamadaba*

Tamaraceite

When driving from Las Palmas to Teror, the town of pilgrimage in the northern central portion of the island, one will pass through Tamaraceite in the northeast. This town makes a paltry and neglected impression. The wealth brought to Gran Canaria by the tourism has seemed to passed Tamaraceite by com-

Picturesque: the town of Tejeda perched on a mountainside

pletely. Tamaraceite is one of the least developed portions of the greater Las Palmas area.

Important Addresses:

Post Office, Police Station, Pharmacy and Doctor's Office, Banco del Bilbao and Banco Español (Currency Exchange): All are located on the main thoroughfare Cruz del Olvajo.

Service Station: On the intersection of the roads to Arucas and Teror.

Restaurants: Pizzeria "Da Massimo" and Bar-Restaurante "Herradura," both located on Cruz del Olvajo.

Tasarte

A small road leads down to Tasarte in the canyon (Barranco de Tasarte), when driving from the turnoff to Veneguera past the green cliffs of Fuente de los Azulejos heading north. This village is larger than Veneguera in the neighbouring canyon. The residents make their livelihood by farming onions and tomatoes. In addition — a rarity on the Canary Islands — the is a larger Protestant congregation, which built a church here in 1988.

After 12 more strenuous kilometres (7½ miles) one will come to the beach of Tasarte with its fine sand.

Restaurants and Bars: Bar-Restaurante "Victoria," Calle Palillo. Bar-Restaurante "Tasarte," Calle Llano.

Tauro

Tauro is a small town northwest of Puerto Rico, approaching from the coastal road between Playa de Amadores and Playa de Mogan. The campsite "Guantanamo" lies two kilometres (1¼ miles) inland. This campsite has become so popular in the past few years that it was necessary to build two additional campsites (Anexo I and Anexo II) on the coast near Playa de Tauro. Now these three campsites can accommodate 1,500 visitors and are open the entire year. The price for three persons with a camping bus, including electricity is around £3.70 ($6.50) per day. There are showers, a recreation centre and a sports field. The road to the older campsite Guantanamo is very dusty, but less so in the campsite itself. The campsite has a number of trees, making it a pleasant, shady oasis. For this reason, many campers can accept the long walk to the beach. The campsite can be contacted by phoning Tel: 27 17 01.

Tejeda

Two kilometres (1¼ miles) from the stone cross Cruz de Tejeda and the Parador Nacional de Tejeda heading toward San Bartolome lies the city of Tejeda where the houses are in part built into the earth in Guanche style. Only the front walls protrude from the earth. The road to Tejeda has a number of observation point, making it possible to take advantage of the fabulous vistas over the mountain range and canyons — especially worth experiencing is the view of the steep Roque Bentaiga.

To get to Tejeda, one must drive down the road to San Bartolome. Beyond the "Albatros" discotheque, in a region rich with almond trees, one will come to the intersection with a service station and a cactus shop. To the right, the road continues to Tejeda. In the centre of town is the Nuestra Señora de Soccoro de Tejeda Church. The benevolent Virgin Mary is depicted by a statue, which is not only venerated, but also guarded as a jewel. Hardly any tourists are aware of this statue. The residents of Tejeda make their living by farming the terraced fields on the mountain slopes. A surprising number of orange trees and prickly-pears grow in this region. There is also a surprising number of begging children.

Tejeda / **Practical Information**

Accommodation: Hotel-Residencia "Tejeda"*, Calle Dr. Domingo Hernandez Guerra 21, Tel: 65 80 55. Seven tidy rooms. Single rooms from £11 ($20); doubles from £13.50 ($24).

Currency Exchange: Caja Insular, Calle Dr. Domingo Fernandez Guerra.

Post Office: Calle Dr. Leocardio Gabrera.

Restaurants

Bar-Restaurante "Gaifa," Calle Dr. Domingo Fernandez Guerra. Recommended for pork and beef dishes as well as locally produced cheese. Complete meals from £7 ($12).

Offering the same selection at the same prices: Bar-Restaurante "Tejeda."

Telephones: On the Plaza in front of the Nuestra Señora Soccoro de Tejeda Church.

Telde

Telde is accessible via the Avenida Maritima and the Autopista de San Cristobal when coming from Las Palmas. 37,000 people live in this, the second largest city on the island. It is simultaneously the most important city in the southern region of Gran Canaria.

The San Juan de Bautista Church was built from volcanic rock of various colours and is definitely worth seeing. Inside, a Flemish altar (15th century) with gold plated wooden carvings depicts the life of Mary. The altar can be considered the most valuable artifact on the island. The altar has six panels with over 70 figures. The life-size statue of Christ above the main altar is a "Tarasco" work and was made in the 16th century by Mexican Indians using corn cobs. This technique is no longer in practice. Although the figure is life-size, it only weighs less than six kilograms (13 pounds).

One can best get to the San Juan de Bautista from Las Palmas by parking at the Plaza, about 500 metres (550 yards) outside the city. In the city of Telde, it is difficult to find a parking space due to the large number of visitors.

The church directly in the centre of the city is even more impressive than the San Juan de Bautista Church. It can only be visited during the afternoon.

Important Addresses

Accommodation: Hotel "Bahia Mar"****. Urbanización La Estrella, Tel: 69 16 41, Fax: 69 69 64, double rooms from £34 ($59).

Currency Exchange: Banco Español, Avenida Gonzales and Caja Insular.

Dentist: Calle Poeta Fernando.

Iberia/Trasmediterranea: Calle Cervantes, across from the church.

Pharmacy: Calle Maria E. Navarro.

Police: Calle Ynes Chinida.

Service Station: Located on the traffic circle.

Taxi: Plaza San Juan, Tel: 4 99.

The diversity is immense in the bird sanctuary and botanical park of Palmitos

Telephones

When placing an international call: dial 07, then wait for a high-pitched tone, and continue by dialling the country code and the number.
Country Codes: United Kingdom — 07.44; United States — 07.1
It can take a while for the connection to be established. International calls can be placed from telephone booths marked "internacionales." One must, however, carry a large amount of change. Newer telephone booths also accept telephone cards. A two-minute call to Europe costs around £1.50 ($2.65) *(→Postal System)*.

Temisas

The campsite Temisas, on the crest of the Lomo de la Cruz mountain, is not far from the 912 metre high (2,982 feet) Teheraj, and is 25 kilometres (16 miles) from Las Palmas. One can get here via the winding road north of the GC 815, which connects Agüimes and Santa Lucia.
At an elevation of 275 metres (900 feet) and exposed to the intense rays of the sun, a barren camping area can accommodate 50 tents or camping buses. The campsite can be contacted by phoning Tel: 24 17 01.

The fluorescent yellow of the Barranco vegetation

What makes tenting in Temisas so attractive is the extremely secluded location. In fact, it is so secluded that only the fewest can stand the solitude for longer periods of time. The nearest beach on the western coast is 12 kilometres (7½ miles) away via Agüimes. There is no bus service, and the road leading by the campground has so little traffic that even the most diligent of hitchhikers will be frustrated. The campsite is open all year.

Teror

The Basilica Nuestra Señora del Pino with the famous Madonna, the island's patron saint, is located in the Teror, the town of pilgrimage south of Arucas. Thousands of pilgrims visit Teror each year at the beginning of September to see the Madonna, who reportedly appeared in the branches of a pine tree on September 8, 1481. The Madonna's robe glistens with pearls and precious stones, sewn onto the material as gifts from pious pilgrims or the affluent residents of this city of 11,000. Those who would like to see the Madonna up close must pay 14p (25 cents) admission. The Madonna my not be photographed; however, one can visit the Cathedral treasure room with its valuable bishop's robes. Those who by all means want a picture of the Madonna must photograph it from the nave. This does require a powerful telephoto lens and a tripod, or at least a very stable hand.

One of the most prominent visitors to the basilica was Pope Pius XII, who visited the Madonna del Pino in 1934. The group of thieves, who stole some of the valuable jewellry were less welcome. The plaza in front of the church housing this sacred relic is lined with souvenir shops. The shops sell mainly embroidered textiles and lace articles. Between the Gallery Georg Heidrich and the basilica is the Casa Museo de Nuestra Señora del Pino, formerly Casa Manrique de Lara. This is the only local museum on Gran Canaria, and it was built in the 17th century. Admission: £34p (60 cents); open daily from 9 am to 1 pm and 4 to 8 pm.

Other sights in Teror: the *Bishop's Palace,* the historical *town hall,* the *Zister Zienser Monetary* and the *Dominican Monastery.*

The town centre with its interesting buildings can be found by following the signs to the basilica. One will pass by houses built during the colonial period.

Teror / **Practical Information**
Entertainment
"Star" Discotheque, Paseo Gonzales Diaz.
"Calypso" Discotheque, below the basilica.

Important Addresses
Bus Terminal: Near the service station in the centre of town.
Police Station: Near the San Matias Abbey.
Restaurants
Restaurante "Eidetesa," located to the left when entering town coming from Miraflor. A remote restaurant, in which one can enjoy a quiet meal or snack. Restaurante "San Matias," shortly after leaving town toward Arucas, Tel: 63 07 65. Tour groups making a stop in Teror visit this restaurant. It has remained inexpensive despite this demand. For about £7 ($12), good food is served in generous portions.

Theatre →*Entertainment*

Theft

Although the Canary islands are among the most frequently visited holiday destinations for middle and northern Europeans, this has hardly led to an increase in crime. Even in the larger centres on Tenerife and Gran Canaria, there is little to criticise.
One qualification: Las Palmas de Gran Canaria. It is a big city with marked social contrasts. Owing to the fact that Las Palmas is one of the largest harbours in Europe, it consistently attracts illegal immigrants. They can blend in well among all of the tourists here. The principles of a big city are in effect in Las Palmas. Leaving a rental car unlocked is ill-advised. Even leaving luggage in a locked car is not a good idea.
Hotels will usually offer the use of a safe in which valuables can be deposited. Expensive articles should by all means be stored in a safe, even if this service does cost a few extra pesetas per day. The peace of mind is well worth the extra money. Travel insurance covering theft is also recommended, in case something is stolen despite the precautions (→*Insurance*).
→*Behaviour, Embassies and Consulates, Police*

Time of Day

The clocks seem to run differently on the Canary Islands. For instance, dinner is served quite late, although the population has meanwhile adapted to the tourists — dinner is now also served somewhat earlier. From 1 to 4 pm is the siesta time — a compensation for the late meal times. It can happen that in the early afternoon shops are closed — this is even true for the churches. The time of day on the Canary Island is one hour later than in Central Europe (Greenwich Mean Time). During the summer, they also go onto summer time, maintaining a one-hour difference with the Spanish Mainland.

Tipping

As a general rule, hotels add 15% to the total amount for service. Waiters, porters, room service and maid service do expect a tip. 15% should serve as orientation in restaurants. Tipping is an acknowledgement of good service — poor service should not be rewarded, even if this does not please the waiter or the establishment.

Also tipped are : taxi drivers, camel guides, ushers in cinemas and theatres and also the curators and supervisors at various points of interest.

Tirajana →*San Bartolome de Tirajana*

Toilets

There are very few public toilets on the Canary Islands. Those in a pinch should not hesitate to go into one of the numerous bars. Those who find this brash can clear their conscience by ordering an espresso. This usually costs less than 17p (30 cents). Some bar owners lock the facilities, when they realise that their customers make a "relieved" impression, but the cash register remains empty — understandable enough.

There are two types of toilets on the Canary Islands: the type to sit on and the type to squat above. Both have their advantages and their drawbacks. Beside the toilet is usually a bin, not only used for sanitary napkins and tampons. Toilet paper should not be flushed down the toilet but should be placed in this bin. This can take some getting used to. However, this does prevent the pipes from stopping up. Water is scarce on the islands, and the water pressure is usually insufficient.

Tourist Information

Information can be obtained from the Spanish Tourist Information Offices:
In Great Britain
57-58 Saint James Street
London
SW1 1DL
Tel: (01) 499 09 01
In Las Palmas de Gran Canaria
Provincial Delegation of Information, Triana 70, Tel: 21 87 65.
Touristic Information Bureau, Casa del Tourismo, Parque Santa Catalina, Tel: 26 46 23.
Provincial Ministry for Information, Casa del Tourismo, Parque Santa Catalina, Tel: 27 07 90 and 27 16 00.

Centro de Iniciativas y Tourismo Pueblo Canario, Parque Doramas, Tel: 24 39 93.
Tourist Information Patronage of the Province, Leon y Castillo 17, Tel: 36 24 22 and 36 22 22.

In Playa del Ingles
On the Corner of Avenida de Estados Unidos and Avenida España (near the Yumbo Centre).

Traffic Regulations

One is only allowed to parallel park in the direction of traffic. When parking in a one way street, on even numbered days, one must park on the side of the street with the even house numbers, otherwise on the other side.

Many of the traffic regulations are similar to those in other countries, but the regulation giving the vehicle coming from the right the right of way can be applied more often — especially on traffic circles. At night, vehicles may only drive with low-beams, at dusk with parking lights other than on the throughways and motorways.

One is not only allowed to honk the horn when driving into a curve, one should do this as well for one's own safety. Horn honking is prohibited in cities between 11 pm and 6 am.

There is still no breakdown service available and towing with private vehicles is prohibited. Vehicles which have broken down must be towed by towing companies.

It is not allowed to overtake cars on streets or 100 metres (110 yard) before streets with a visibility of less than 200 metres (220 yards).

A driver who sticks his left hand out of the window is signalling that he or she is stopping for pedestrians.

Travel Documents

For a stay of up to 90 days, citizens of EC member states need only valid identity card to enter Gran Canaria; all other visitors must have a valid passport. When travelling by car, one should always carry a passport; should a police officer request identification, it is better to have it along than saying it is in the hotel. A passport is also required in the following situations: cashing traveller's cheques (or Eurocheques), checking into hotels or other accommodation, registering with the police (when staying longer than 90 days) and when renting a car. A national driving licence and an international insurance card is necessary when bringing one's own car to the Canary Islands. Those who wish to bring pets along must have health certification for the animal or at least proof of rabies vaccination translated into Spanish. The vaccination must have taken place at least 30 days and at most one year prior to entering the Canary Islands. This certification must be notarised by a Spanish consulate before departure *(→Embassies)*. Documents for pets which has not been notarised is only accepted if issued by a governmental or officially recognised veterinarian.

Travel on Gran Canaria

The most comfortable way of getting around on Gran Canaria is by car *(→Car Rental)* since the *→buses* do not always operate regularly and do not go to every town that one might want to visit. Those who bring their own car or motorcycle will need an international insurance car and will also have to affix a nationality sticker to the vehicle.

In the larger towns there is always at least one service station. The fuel supply is sufficient. The service stations are closed on Sundays and holidays. Those who would like to avoid unpleasant surprises should always fill the fuel tank before the weekend.

Fuel prices per litre: normal 92 octane = 30p (53 cents); super 97 octane = 35p (60 cents); diesel (gasoleo "A") = 17p (30 cents). Hitchhiking is always a matter of luck, even on Gran Canaria.

There is no train on any of the Canary Islands, but there are quite a few taxi drivers. A taxi will charge a flat rate of £1.50 ($2.65); for a longer trip, 30p (53 cents) per kilometre. The taxis in the northern parts of Gran Canaria will, as a rule, be equipped with a meter; taxis in the southern regions might not. For longer stretches and self-planned routes, one should agree upon a price in advance. A few approximate examples from Playa del Ingles:

To San Agustin: £3.10 ($5.40)
To Maspalomas: £3.40 ($5.90)
To Las Palmas: £21.70 ($38.25)
To Puerto Rico: £10 ($17.65)
To the airport: £13.35 ($23.50)

There are two options to travel to the neighbouring islands: Iberia Airlines flights or Trasmediterranea ships. Iberia has daily flights from Gran Canaria to Tenerife, Fuerteventura and Lanzarote. From Tenerife, there are flights to La Palma and El Hierro. A one-way ticket to the neighbouring islands costs about £20 ($36). The ships are somewhat less expensive. Ships depart daily from Gran Canaria's Puerto de la Luz *(→Las Palmas)*; on Mondays, Tuesdays, Thursdays and Sundays, there are ships departing to Arrecife on Lanzarote with one stop at Puerto del Rosario on Fuerteventura. Wednesdays and Fridays, ships depart for Santa Cruz de la Palma and Hierro via Tenerife. A one-way trip to a neighbouring island costs around £17 ($30). In addition, one can also take the jet foil to the second harbour on Fuerteventura Morro Jable. The trip lasts 90 minutes and costs around £24 ($42) for the one-way trip.

Travelling to Gran Canaria

From London, a flight to Las Palmas International Airport costs around £220 ($380) depending on the season and based on a stay of up to one month. If staying longer, the flight can increase by about £65 ($115). Charter flights usually require that the date of the return flight is set in advanced. These flights are usually booked as part of a package tour, meaning that accommodation is also included. One is less committed with "camping flights," which include hotel vouchers: one can then arrange accommodation after arriving on Gran Canaria. The trip to Las Palmas by ship from Cadiz in southern Spain via Tenerife takes about two and a half days (approximately 800 nautical miles). This does offer one advantage in that an automobile can also be transported. This costs between £67 ($118) and £170 ($295) depending on the length of the vehicle with an additional charge of between £100 ($177) and £170 ($295) per person (children pay half of the adult fare). The ferry from Cadiz to Tenerife and Gran Canaria operates three times a week during the summer months; otherwise, only once a week. The current schedule for departures and prices can be obtained from travel agencies, who will also be able to arrange bookings. With the exception of La Gomera, all of the Canary Islands have airports. Gran Canaria is also readily accessible by air from the neighbouring islands (→ *Travel on Gran Canaria*). The harbour of Las Palmas can be reached by ferry from all of the Canary Islands. The ship line offering this service is the Compañia Trasmediterranea Aucona, with offices located on each of the harbours served.

Vaccinations

No vaccinations are necessary when travelling to the Canary Islands. However, it cannot hurt to check when the last tetanus shot took place, since one can easily injure one's feet in the lava fields, in Malpaises or even on the beaches.

Valleseco

Valleseco is a lovely village, halfway between Teror and Cruz de Tejeda. The town church is, San Vicente, is especially fascinating because of its ceiling comprised of several domes. It is located on Calle Leon y Castillo, near the Bar-Restaurante "La Herradura" and the Cafetería "Micielo."

A service station can be found on the Corner of Calle Juan Narrero Diaz. 3,000 people live in Valleseco and the surrounding regions; the main source of income is the production of oranges and lemons.

Vecindario

The town of Vecindario lies on the road running parallel to the motorway from Las Palmas to Playa del Ingles in the southern region of the island. It is comprised of only a few houses along the main street. However, in almost all of these houses, there are shops — from video shops, to electrical appliance stores and even music shops. It is not a terribly inviting town; however, there are two guest houses here which could be of interest when travelling through. Guest House "Casa Paco," Calle Presidente Zarate, Tel: 75 34 42, £11 ($20) for two persons.

In addition, there is a guest house with no name on Avenida de Canarias 260.

Vega de San Mateo →*San Mateo*

Vegetation

"Cardon" is the term used to describe *spurge plants,* which have the appearance of a candelabra. Some passers-by assume these to be cactus plants. These plants contain a large quantity of poisonous juice in their roots, fruit and branches, which is at the very least an eye irritant. The juice is said to have been used in the embalming of the Canarian mummies. A spurge plant grow up to 10 feet in diameter. It grows on all of the larger Canary Islands; however, not on the coast.

In 1820, the cochineal lice and the prickly pear were imported from Mexico. The cochineal produce a pigment used in the production of cosmetics. The farmers on the island feared that these lice would contaminate the feed for their livestock.

However, the cochineal were a true blessing for the islands: between 1831 and 1870, the export of this pigment producing louse increased from four kilograms to 300 metric tons. This was one fifth of the world production behind Guatemala and Mexico. In 1877, it sank to 220 metric tons; in 1911, only small amounts were exported via Marseille to China. Since the end of the Second World War, twelve metric tons of cochineal are used in the production of cosmetics. Today, only traces of this pigment can still be found in lipstick and other cosmetics. The Canary Islands produce enough of this pigment to meet the entire demand in Europe.

After the lice went out of fashion, the *banana* was the export hit. Banana liqueur is one of the island's specialities.

Cinerarias, chrysanthemums, succulent plants and *"viper heads"* (there are giant red-blossomed specimens on Tenerife) also grow on the islands — even sweet lemons grow here.

Fig, acacia and *eucalyptus trees* were imported. The eucalyptus trees from Australia were mainly used to line the streets. The Acacia trees originate from South Africa or Australia, and the fig trees come from Australia, Africa, Asia or America.

Veneguera

Veneguera, or Las Casas de Veneguera, is a village north of Mogan when driving on the GC 810 and turning left toward the coast after about 8 kilometres (5 miles). The town is at the beginning of the Veneguera canyon. This is where the largest specimens of the spurge plants (→ *Vegetation*) are found. In the form of a candelabra, they grow to a height of over 5 metres (14 feet). Veneguera itself is a small town, which only very few travellers visit. In the bar "Las Cañadas" one can empty a bottle of wine with the owner in a very friendly atmosphere.

The end of this idyllic atmosphere is in sight. It is 12 kilometres (8 miles) from Veneguera to the coast and a good road through the banana, orange, papaya and lemon plantations has not yet been built. Earth moving equipment and bulldozers have already levelled the entire fishing harbour with the exception of two buildings. As it looks, yet another tourist centre, characteristic of Gran Canaria's west coast, will probably be built up along this bay.

Water

The water supply is one of the largest problems on the Canary Islands. Meanwhile, the tour organisations always point out that water shortages are possible. The major burden on the water supply is tourism. However, it is by no means so bad that the wells have run dry. The number of those using the water has doubled due to tourism.

In the early colonial period, water was still considered property of the privileged. Today, the allocation of the water is overseen by the "herades" which have been in existence on Gran Canaria since 1505. Surface water is used in agriculture and for the everyday demands of the populace.

However, especially on Tenerife in the Orotava Valley, in Cumbre de Pedro Gil, Candelaria and Güimar, there are "gallerias." The tunnels are around 5 feet high and are tunnelled to the ground water supply in the mountains. Most are

¼ to ½ mile long but they can measure up to 2½ miles (4 kilometres) in length. The total length of the gallerias network on Tenerife is estimated at 630 miles (1,000 kilometres). Building these tunnels is a risk — some never contain water. Others, like the tunnels of Güimar on Tenerife, in contrast, contain so much water that they can supply the southern portion of the island via the "Canal de Sur."

In addition, there are deep wells ("pozos"). Motorised or wind-driven pumps bring water to the surface of Gran Canaria, Fuerteventura, Tenerife, La Gomera and La Palma from a depth of over 300 metres.

The largest reservoirs the "presas," can be found on Fuerteventura — the "Embalse de los Moninos;" and in the southwestern region of Gran Canaria — "Presa de la Chira" and "Presa de la Ayagaures."

Weights and Measures

On the Canary Islands, the metric system is used, including degrees Celsius.

Youth Hostels →*Accommodation*